Frances R. (Frances Rose) Howe

A visit to Bois d'Haine, the home of Louise Lateau

Frances R. (Frances Rose) Howe

A visit to Bois d'Haine, the home of Louise Lateau

ISBN/EAN: 9783742869821

Manufactured in Europe, USA, Canada, Australia, Japa

Cover: Foto ©Lupo / pixelio.de

Manufactured and distributed by brebook publishing software (www.brebook.com)

Frances R. (Frances Rose) Howe

A visit to Bois d'Haine, the home of Louise Lateau

The Seraphim are the highest among the angelic hosts. They are resplendent with the fires of Divine Charity—Chiefs of the first hierarchy, at the head of the celestial squadrons, they command the invincible army of which the Lord is God.

God has deigned to teach us that He has established the most admirable order among angels. The angels form three hierarchies, each one composed of three choirs, making nine choirs of angels—Seraphim, Cherubim, Thrones—Powers, Principalities, Dominations—Virtues, Archangels, Angels.

They are distinguished above all by the burning fire of ardent charity which consumes them, and transmits to all the other angels the pure love of God which captivates eternally. They draw from the source itself in the Divine Essence this immense love which keeps them lost in the Presence of God.

S. + P.

SERAPH.

ISAIAS VI. 2.

Nearest to Him, they dare not raise their eyes towards His Holy Countenance, nor to regard Its splendors, being scarcely able to sustain themselves in the presence of so much Majesty.

"I am seized with an intense, a vivid sense of the presence of God. I see His immensity and my own nothingness, and I know not where to hide myself."—LOUISE LATEAU.

A VISIT TO BOIS D'HAINE,

THE HOME OF LOUISE LATEAU.

REVISED FROM THE "AVE MARIA."

By FRANCES R. HOWE.

Sapiate che l'esercitio del patire è cosa tanto pregiata e nobile che il Verbo, trovandosi nel Seno dell suo eterno Padre abondantissime di richezze e delitie di Paradiso, perche non era ornato della Stola del patire, venne in terra per questo ornamento, e questo era Dio e non si potea ingannare.—*St. Mary Magdalen of Pazzi.*

BALTIMORE:
KELLY, PIET AND COMPANY.
1878.

TO MY DEAR AUNT,

Mother Mary Cecilia,

AND TO

MY INSTRUCTRESSES AND MY SCHOOLMATES,

THE

TEACHERS AND PUPILS

OF

ST. MARY'S INSTITUTE, VIGO COUNTY, INDIANA,

THIS VOLUME

IS MOST AFFECTIONATLY DEDICATED.

INTRODUCTION.

A LONG time has elapsed since our visit to Bois d'Haine, and its events have lost that freshness which gives a portion of the charm of novelty to a narrative whose facts are of recent occurrence; nevertheless the delay in bringing it before the public has not been without profitable results. Five years sojourn amid scenes of a Catholicism, a Christianity, whose vigorous vitality passes the understanding of the mere tourist, which, in order to appreciate, one must dwell amidst, had unfitted us more than we knew for comprehending the effect which would be produced on the Catholics of the New World by hearing the wonderful life of Louise Lateau, the Stigmatica of Bois d'Haine. During the past three years ample opportunities have arisen before us of discovering the different shades of feeling aroused in the hearts and minds of American Catholics by a description of that, which may be witnessed at Bois d'Haine, and the endeavor of the succeeding pages will be to explain those features of the case, which perplex the Catholics of this country.

This little work addresses itself solely to Catholics, therefore arguments are selected presupposing that the reader acknowledges that in the Catholic Church alone is found the true interpretation of Scripture. However, others are welcome to peruse it and gain whatever ideas they can therefrom. In general terms, it may be stated that those ignorant of our faith obtain at least as much instruction from books intended to teach us what we do believe, as they do from those which are compiled especially for them, and which, too often, are full of unauthorized denials and unwarranted admissions. The aim of this work is two-fold: to explain the utility of Louise's sufferings, and to give a clear and concise idea of her condition. By dilating on the doctrine of expiatory suffering, the necessity of her condition is shown, and the almost universal question concerning her—which is not, "Does she really suffer?" but, "Why does she suffer?" is fully answered.

In order to give a clear and concise idea of the miracles of her life, any detail that does not bear directly on the subject is omitted. Of her previous life a few items only are selected—striking ones—that will give a just impression of her real character, and help to remove the idea that contemplative vocations render their possessors careless of the woes of others, and useless to their fellow-beings. It is not proposed to supplant the other works on this subject, but merely to hereby form an introduction to them. If, after reading this, anyone should desire fuller details, they can be found in the works of Dr. Lefebvre on Louise Lateau; or, perhaps, in a form more pleasing to the general reader, in a charming work by Doctor Imbert-Gourbeyre, professor at the medical college of Clermont-Ferrand, entitled "Les Stigmatisées." If it has not been yet translated into English, it is a matter of regret. All Louise's illnesses, previous to the spring of 1868, have been mentioned in the following pages, to show what was her general physical condition before the appearance of the miracle; but the mass of medical proof, and the details of experiments with which the generality of works on Louise Lateau are filled, are omitted in this. They have been repeated sufficiently by other writers, and this does not aspire to be a handbook of medical science.

In order to give as true an idea as possible of Louise's condition, her life has been still more condensed, and presented to the reader in a form similar to that of a chronological table, and so arranged as to serve as an index. At present Louise's state of Stigmatization is continual, but it is difficult to obtain a trustworthy account of the manner in which the change took place, or of the exact date of its occurrence. Of this much we are certain, that since the year 1876 she has been unable to leave her room, and that the Holy Communion has since then been brought to her daily, but we have not been able to procure the precise dates of these events, so as to place them in this index. The reports that used to reach America from time to time three years ago, that Louise Lateau was in a dying condition, arose from a misapprehension of her state; it was difficult to persuade the American public that her helplessness and suffering were then confined to Friday, and that was one important phase of the miracle which ought to be well understood. Having once explained to the world that Louise was well and strong on six days out of seven, Dr. Lefebvre thought that, while telling the events of each Friday that he visited Bois d'Haine, he would not be misunderstood, even if he did not repeat each time that the next day found her again in health.

The conduct of Louise's family is not recounted in an idle spirit of gossip, but principally to show how very unjust it is to suppose that they desire or in any way occasion Louise's sufferings. Perhaps it will be necessary to explain to some that our own experiences are made so prominent for a serious object, and that particulars concerning those who were admitted at the same time with ourselves are not inserted just to take up space. We have striven to make everything seem as real as possible. We have wished to impress the reader with the fact that persons, who, like himself, can be fatigued and travel-worn, who are obliged to eat, drink, and sleep, have entered Louise's cottage and have seen the evidences of her wonderful life.

Whenever in these pages the word ecstasy is found, it is used in its ordinary colloquial sense; that is, as the name of a trance occasioned by religious and supernatural causes; at the same time the ordinary reader should be informed, that, to use the word in its proper sense, requires a thorough knowledge of metaphysics. Four years ago Louise had not yet arrived at true ecstasy; her state of mental withdrawing from her surroundings was, in the language of the schools, merely spiritual slumber.

The Catholic reader need not fear that the Scriptural quotations, which he finds applied in a manner new to him, are suffering a distortion of meaning, the result of the writer's own inventive powers. Those applied as referring to Stigmatization are copied from inscriptions frequently found in churches, chapels, and oratories dedicated to St. Francis of Assisi. Such texts as are used to prove the existence of the possibility of total abstinence from all food, and of the power of the Holy Eucharist to nourish, are found thus applied in the authentic lives of such saints and holy persons as St. Catherine of Sienna, Blessed Nicholas von der Flüe.

Among other false ideas prevalent here concerning the miracle of Bois d'Haine there is one which calls it a supernatural exhibition, merely local in point of time; that is, that Louise's condition is but a portion of the wonderful events of the present day—her Stigmatization an unusual miracle, which, when the need of her expiatory existence has passed away, will cease to be, and those who hold this idea suppose that, when she dies, she will leave no successor on this throne of suffering. Inasmuch as there is always sin, and always will be as long as time endures, the need of such as she is continual, besides we have no reason to suppose that she is the last mortal destined to join the choir of Seraphim. That she is not an isolated case, but that she belongs to a dynasty unbroken since the days of St. Francis of Assisi, may be seen by referring to the carefully prepared list of authentic cases of Stigmatization in "Les Stigmatisées," by Dr. Imbert-Gourbeyre. We may believe, if we wish—and how much better we would often be employed if we were trying to discover what we might believe, instead of seeking to find out what we need not believe!—that there has been no interregnum in this dynasty of seraphic souls during all the eighteen centuries of Christianity; that St. Francis of Assisi was only chosen to exhibit visibly to the world that which had hitherto, perhaps, been invisible or hidden in the cells of the Fathers of the Desert.

The reason of the error, stated in the preceding paragraph, is apparent: we had borrowed some high sounding phrases from heresy, among them, "the age of miracles has passed away." We liked this sentence, it was difficult to relinquish it, and when modern miracles were flung in our midst, we said the age of miracles has been renewed. Miracles have been multiplied and redoubled in these times, but they had never ceased; they were continuous in Italy, Spain, and Catholic Germany, miracles both small and great; now and then an instantaneous one shining out amid the many gradual ones, but what was that to the world? Other nations talked vaguely of "corruptions," "degrading superstitions," etc., etc. But at last, like a stream of moving lava, the supernatural burst these barriers, and, spreading over the Christian world, obliged all Catholics to remember that Christ had said, "I am with you even unto the end," then we exclaim, miracles have recommenced! As well might one, who had led years of a Casper Hauser existence, exclaim, on merging from his cellar-like dungeon, the sun has recommenced to shine!

There is a certain class of Catholics who pride themselves on their incredulity with regard to supernatural events; they think themselves quite superior to those who are glad to learn that there are visible links between mankind and heaven. Many of these Catholics dwell far removed from the fountain-heads of our holy religion, and they seldom have occasion to think of the supernatural lives led by God's holy ones, so they measure holiness by strange standards. They love to hear of what the saints have done for their fellow men, and they care very little about the wonders which God has worked in His saints; nay, if God has repaid the devotion of any one of his servants in an extraordinary manner, the reward which has been bestowed inspires them with—there is no other word for it—a disgust for that saint. Such as Louise Lateau they fling aside. In vain we show them that she has visited the sick and even buried the dead; she stole from her moments of leisure to give time to prayer and contemplation, and, as she really loved her neighbor for God's sake, He deigned to manifest His power in her, so, in their eyes, her life was no longer active—no longer useful. It would be hard to convince these persons that they are substituting philanthropy for the love of God, and that, however much the working saints, as they love to style their favorites, alleviated suffering purely for the love of God, their admiration of these saints springs from an entirely different motive, a compound of selfishness and self-love.

These are the Catholics who are always seeking to learn what they need not believe, who are always telling those outside of the Church that it is very possible to be a good Catholic and not believe this or that. It is very possible to be a good priest or a good bishop, and to be extremely cautious about admitting the miraculous nature of every unusual event; in fact, this caution is a part of the vocation of the clergy; it is their duty to us to carefully sift every particle of evidence before they place an event among probable facts which we may believe if we wish. To be a good Catholic layman and to be perpetually doubting everything save what we are strictly obliged to believe, is a difficult task—one rarely accomplished. We will almost invariably find that the Catholic who labors strenuously to believe nothing save the bare articles of faith, finds great difficulty in accepting even these. We cannot deny, of course, that God is so good as not to require from us acquiescence in anything save these bare articles of faith, but even if we do not incur his anger by refusing our credence to miraculous events, we must not imagine that our incredulity makes us better Catholics, advances us on the road of perfection, or renders us more pleasing to God.

Without dwelling on the incongruity of professing to believe in the possibility of miracles, and afterwards doubting every miracle presented to our notice, even when accompanied by an amount of evidence much more overwhelming than that by which we would willingly see a fellow-being condemned to prison or death, we ought to consider seriously within ourselves and ask a question similar to that propounded by Father Faber, in " All for Jesus," when he inquired for the ravages made by enthusiasm among the English Catholics of his day. Where will we find the ravages made among us American Catholics by too great credulity in matters appertaining to the Blessed Virgin and the saints? Just where Father Faber found the ravages made by enthusiasm.

We can hardly find among ourselves that phase of the love of the marvellous which St. Jane Frances sought to eradicate in her daughters. Had these had the slightest doubts concerning the reality of the miracles which she did not permit to be read aloud in the refectory or at their spiritual conferences, we may be sure that she would have said, "in this I praise you not." Very few of us have reached that stage of piety where we need to be reproved for meditating too frequently on the miraculous side of the lives of the saints. It is true, there is one style of the love of the marvellous among us, but that is to be conquered by careful explanations concerning miracles, and those who would wish to see Louise Lateau from mere idle curiosity may learn, from the difficulties besetting our path, that Bois d'Haine is not a museum, but a pilgrimage. Although not as yet enriched by the special indulgences conceded to shrines, all who visit it piously will receive the graces merited by those who meditate earnestly on the Passion of our Lord.

A
VISIT TO BOIS D'HAINE,

THE HOME OF LOUISE LATEAU.

I.

DURING the month of April, 1873, one of our party was received among the pupils of the Benedictines of the Blessed Sacrament in Paris, the object being the study and practice of the French language. Separated by the cloister from all the temptations and dangers of the world, the good religieuses are enabled to comprehend more clearly the condition of the Church militant, and they are thoroughly informed concerning the progress of Christianity; and kindred subjects are always the theme of their conversation at times when their rule does not enjoin silence. While the young lady was with them, she one day entered a room at the close of an animated recital of events of a miraculous nature, just given by one of the pupils to a nun.

"*Tiens*," said the nun, as she turned to address the new-comer, " you who visit Catholic countries to learn whatever is instructive and edifying, here is something that you ought to witness. There is at present in Belgium a young girl who has the stigmata and suffers the Agony of the Passion every Friday."

" Is the world at large, are the laity, admitted?" was the natural inquiry.

" Oh certainly; and you would have no difficulty, coming, as you do, from so far," was the reply.

The art of Italy, in church and gallery, in painting and sculpture, had made the sacred wounds of St. Francis of Assisi a thing less of faith than of sight, therefore the account of the Belgian Stigmatica was readily accepted by the young lady without the least emotion of doubt.

As to a desire to behold so great a miracle, it seemed to her a species of irreverent curiosity; the words of Our Lord, "Blessed are they who have not seen and yet have believed," rang in her ears, and so, without thinking of expressing a wish to make either herself or any other member of her family a witness of the miracle, she merely related it to them as a great favor vouchsafed by the Almighty to reassure and comfort His faithful children.

In the midst of the many supernatural facts with which the present history of the Church is no less replete than it was in former ages, the subject had ceased to occupy our thoughts and conversation, when, during the June of that same year, we met the Very Rev. Father Sorin at Neuilly. While speaking of all the holy ground which one might find in the Old World, he expressed his suprise that we had not visited the Belgian Stigmatica, who was the one at present delegated to show forth vividly that which took place eighteen centuries ago in Gethsemani and on Mt. Calvary. Besides the beautiful legends of St. Francis of Assisi, then so fresh in our minds, we all remembered that, in the first part of this century, Tyrol had been so highly rewarded for her intense devotion to the Way of the Cross, as to have among her people two striking examples of this holy wonder, but of the present case in Belgium we were not so well informed. But as we then had in contemplation another long and arduous journey, the prospects of a tour in Belgium were so very improbable that we did not make minute inquiries concerning the matter. Nevertheless, it was an idea which, dismiss it as we might, was always ready to present itself, haunting us throughout our subsequent travels.

Early in the following spring a vivid dream fastened our attention still more fixedly on the wondrous miracle. For months the dreamer had not thought of the young Stigmatica of Belgium, and yet she seemed to find herself upon the favored spot without knowing by what means. The sufferer was lying in bed, covered up to her chin, manifesting a great annoyance at being seen, but as the dreamer entered, the Stigmatica smiled and drew her bleeding hands from under the coverlid, in order to show them to the stranger. At this the dreamer thought she fell on her knees, awestruck with an overwhelming sense of some unsought, uncomprehended responsibility, and she awoke saying:

"What is it that I must do? What does she see that the Lord wishes me to do that she shows me her wounds, when she so sedulously hides them from others?"

It was broad daylight, and in our semi-military quarter of Genoa, Carignano, the regiments were marching to their morning drill to the sound of merry bugles; the birds mingled their spring warblings with the clear notes that told our hour of rising, but scarcely heeding either, the awakened dreamer began a rapid, excited relation of her sleeping thoughts. We had just learned that circumstances would render it necessary for us to embark from a northern port, in order to return to America, and so we then thought, "Well, we are about to pass near Belgium." But although Belgium is a small kingdom, it is rather a large place in which to search for a person whose name one does not know, for at that time the humble peasant maid of Bois d'Haine had not yet begun to appear on the pages of journals of science. Her name had not as yet become familiar to the world at large, and we only could rely on the probability that everyone in that country must be well informed of the miracle in their midst. At that period, however, the uppermost thought in our minds was a pilgrimage to Our Lady of Lourdes, and that happily accomplished, we returned to Genoa to repose for some days before proceeding on our trans-Alpine journey.

We returned just in time for three beautiful festivals—festivals which perhaps many scarcely remark in this missionary country, but which, nevertheless, commemorate events conveying important lessons to all classes and to all nations, and these three were the festivals of St. Aloysius, St. John the Baptist, and St. Peter and St. Paul. On the 21st of June the altars dedicated to St. Aloysius, of which nearly every Italian church has one, were laden with the choicest flowers—flowers that would be the rarest exotics in our climate—and these beautiful blossoms were all *ex voto* from the young men of Genoa to that model of holy innocence, whom the Church has given to Christian youths as their patron and protector. St. John the Baptist is one of the many patrons, to whose protection and intercession Genoa ascribes her prosperity and wealth, and therefore the feast of his nativity is to them an occasion of great jubilee. Italy is like one vast suburb of Rome—each city echoes the words of infallibility; each city responds faithfully to all its decisions, copies its maternal kindness in placing graces within easy reach, grieves in all its sorrows, shares in all its joys, and thus the 29th of June is celebrated in Genoa with hardly less ecclesiastical pomp than in Rome itself, where it is the great patronal feast of the city.

These numerous festivals of the Catholic Church are just so many means of detaching the heart of man from earth and lifting it heavenward. Spain perhaps excepted, Italy is the only nation on the continent of Europe that acknowledges the necessity of this detachment, for it is only in Italy that we saw the wishes of our Holy Mother, the Church, in this respect properly fulfilled. The assertion that the progress of civilization is retarded by this frequent interruption of worldly affairs, may be met by a simple reference to Italian art and science, for if the word civilization regards the intellectual development of a nation, Italy has certainly a decided advantage. If, however, civilization means an intense self-seeking, consummate attention to bodily comfort and to every thing that can possibly minister thereto, then, of course, the more that Heaven is forgotten, the less that a land is Christian, the higher will be its standard of civilization. We might institute a fair comparison between the knowledge and progress of Italy and her monuments of architecture, those palaces and churches that challenge the admiration of the world, that force praise even from the lips of those whose hearts are filled with hatred of the religion, by the sublime inspirations of which, human genius reached so high a development. Just as these are not frail structures of wood, or of tiny bricks, or of materials that would have seemed mere pebbles in the sight of Solomon and his builders, but are composed of blocks of solid stone, whose size is worthy of the labor of man, set one upon another, firmly, securely, until the edifices rise grand and harmonious, worthy of beings created to the image and likeness of God, so her intellectual progress does not lie in propagating as truths, in which man may more surely trust than in divine revelation, all the mere probabilities of science, all the but half-proven theories of to-day, which to-morrow will be themes of a scorn as unmeasured as the confidence which at one time was placed in them; so her great minds are busied separating in every thing wheat from chaff, truth from falsehood, the probable from the improbable; they earnestly desire to distinguish substance from shadow, and they are certain of ultimate success, because in all creatures they wish to see traces of the hand of the Creator, and to find the evidences of Eternal Truth.

But like many other intellectual pleasures, these festivals, while elevating the mind, weary the body, and thus, although the 30th of June had been appointed as the day of our departure, we decided to remain a day longer, so as to be able to begin our long journey totally free from previous fatigue. We staid the more willingly because our excellent landlord and landlady were so kind and obliging, and we felt that it might be a long time before we would be again as well situated.

"You will begin to think that we are never going," said we to our landlord, as we announced our intention of remaining another day.

"Well, if you wait until I send you away, you won't leave very soon," replied he, merrily; for Italians are very fond of little jests, and none more so than our Genoese landlord.

But we did not wait for him to send us away,

and on the morning of the 1st of July we descended to the dining-room much earlier than usual, for we were to take the eight o'clock train going north. As we seated ourselves around the breakfast table, our landlord handed us a number of the London Daily Telegraph. Laying it on the table, he perpetrated his daily joke of "fresh news," and while the scalding tea was cooling, one of us took up the journal to give a hasty glance at the latest intelligence from Spain and from the Church militant in Prussia. An exclamation from the reader attracted the attention of the others, and in reply to their questions she read aloud a long article headed—

"Louise Lateau, the Stigmatica of Bois d'Haine."

It was a letter from the Berlin correspondent of the Daily Telegraph, who intermingled his own views with translations from an article published in the Germania, the leading Catholic organ of Berlin, by Father Majunke, who had just returned from Bois d'Haine.

Even from the absurdly literal and unfair

translation of peculiar Teutonic idioms, so powerful when coming from the mouth or pen of a German, we could see that, in the original, Father Majunke's account must have been most telling in its logic, as well as vivid in its description. The correspondent closed the article by a vain attempt to conceal the fact that even he had not been able to entirely resist Father Majunke's course of reasoning, saying that "the Rev. gentleman must have a very confiding nature if he expected the intellectual world of Berlin to credit a mediæval myth of that kind." He forgot, however, to define the difference between caricaturing a language and translating word for word its peculiar phrases. We are sure that it is easy to translate the German terms expressing the might and majesty of God very literally without introducing cockney slang. When he penned his description, he had no idea that, intermix as he might with his own sceptical thoughts the great facts on which he was treating, he was doing so great a service to three Catholics, by pointing out the spot of

Europe where they might witness so tremendous a proof of the truth of the Holy Scriptures.

"Oh!" we all exclaimed, "had we left yesterday we might never have learned so accurately where to seek this miracle!"

And we all felt an increase of devotion towards the festivals, whose observance had so fatigued us as to thus fortunately detain us until the arrival of this important information. Perhaps, had we not read this article, we might have been more readily deterred from fulfilling our promise to Very Rev. Father Sorin that, should we ever find ourselves in the neighborhood of Belgium, we would make an effort to become witnesses of this manifestation of the miracle of the Stigmata.

II.

As the weeks passed on, while we traveled slowly northward, the resolution to visit Bois d'Haine became each day more and more defined. The 5th of August found us at Spires, the see of an ancient bishopric. Its cathedral is the St. Denis of Germany; but it is not the tombs of emperors and kings which form the chief interest for the Catholic tourist, neither is it the beautiful architecture of the sacred edifice, but the fact that St. Bernard there, within its walls, gave utterance to that sublime praise of the Mother of God, "*O clemens! O pia! O dulcis Virgo Maria.*"

But to us Spires presented another attraction. Its bishop we had known while he was still abbot of the Convent of St. Boniface in Munich, and not only did we anticipate an agreeable visit, but we also hoped to obtain useful advice concerning a visit to Louise Lateau. We found his residence easily, but when we arrived at the door we met the reception usually given in Germany by those who serve ecclesiastical dignitaries. We were scanned from head to foot, and, deaconnesses no longer existing in the church, three ladies mean only three ciphers as far as religious importance is concerned. Our cards were scrutinized before our faces with a cool impertinence, and if our appearance had partially satisfied the porter that our social position entitled us to pay our respects to his master, our cards, being like the cards of any one then claiming the protection of the American flag, utterly destitute of armorial bearings, he told us, without further inquiry, that at present the bishop was deeply engaged in his daily routine of duty, which could not be interrupted, and that he would not be free until two o'clock. Now, two o'clock is precisely the hour of the departure of the Rhine steamer, usually preferred by those traveling for pleasure to the railway, and as an ecclesiastic in the Cathedral had informed us positively that the morning was the time at which the bishop was free to receive visits, we were not to blame if, in our hearts, we accused the porter of wishing to rid himself of us by mentioning an hour at which it would be impossible for us to come. We may have made a rash judgment, but be that as it may, we relinquished the idea of the steamer, concluding to avail ourselves of the railway train, which left at a much later hour, but which was far less agreeable.

The porter seemed both surprised and vexed to see us when we returned at two o'clock, an hour which was probably as inconvenient to the bishop as it had been to us. He did again attempt to send us away, but finally our repeated assertions, that we were acquainted with the bishop, seemed to make some impression on him, and at last he did consent to carry up the episcopal stairway the cards which he found so basely destitute of any tokens of nobility.

Our difficulties in this case arose from the general ignorance of foreigners, and of Germans in particular, concerning that law of the United States which withheld passports and consular protection from those of her citizens who, while traveling abroad, made use of any of the insignia of nobility. Owing to this law, or to the general lack of knowledge of its existence in Europe, whichever you will, the very passport that told the police that you were not a vagabond, placed you in a very false light as far as social rank is concerned.

The fortress once stormed, the outworks gained, we found that Abbot Hanneberg had not, in becoming Bishop Hanneberg, lost any of that unaffected simplicity of manner which had seemed so charming in the modest, unpretentious reception-room of that architecturally grand convent of St. Boniface. He received us with that same manner. In spite of the episcopal purple, the bishop was at heart still the Benedictine, and the episcopal residence was not half so dear to him as the less conspicuous halls of his own convents in Munich, or at beautiful Andechs, in the picturesque outskirts of the

Bavarian Alps. Since then, God has called him to a home far more beautiful than the one to which he alluded with so much affection in the course of that afternoon's conversation.

The events of the time that had elapsed since we had last seen him having been duly discussed, we spoke of our desire to visit Louise Lateau. He advised us to continue our Rhine journey as far as Cologne, whence we might reach Belgium in a few hours. Bois d'Haine, he informed us, was in the diocese of Tournay, therefore we must apply to the bishop of that see for the requisite permission. He added, if, however, it suited our plans better to go to Mechlin, the archbishop there, being the primate of Belgium, overruled the bishop of Tournay, and that, therefore, his permission would be equally valid. Bringing us maps, he showed us the relative position of these three cities, Cologne, Mechlin, and Tournay, and thus in every thing relating to this proposed visit he exhibited the kindest interest; but, as he was not personally acquainted with either dignitary, he was unable to give us any introductory letter, although he encouraged us to apply, saying that the prelates of Belgium were excessively kind and affable, and that Catholics from America—that missionary country—certainly had claims on the Church of the Old World.

The hope that we would make a better impression on the bishop of Tournay, than we had made on the porter of the episcopal residence of Spire, accompanied us throughout our subsequent journey, and we now determined more firmly than ever to fulfill our promise, which was now more binding, since we had learned so very accurately what to do and where to go. We did not then know that the rude conduct of the porter was simply the commencement of that trial and humiliation—that cross which we carried to the very threshold of the Lateau cottage, and which did not desert us until we were far distant from Bois d'Haine—only the beginning, only a portion of that cross which all must carry who wish to stand on this modern Calvary.

We did not begin to have any conception of the difficulties attending a visit to Louise Lateau until when speaking on the subject to the Rev. Dr. Bellesheim, who occupies the confessional " pro Anglica " in the Cathedral of Cologne, we were told by him that so many were the applications, that only a very small proportion of the applicants could obtain admission to the tiny cottage, adding that the chances of success were slight for those who came unrecommended, he advised us, if we knew any source from which we could obtain an introductory letter, to apply for it immediately. Aside from the promise which we had made, we had a strong feeling that it was the duty of every American Catholic to contribute his or her mite to the multiform missionary work of the New World, and that we had no right to neglect any means of making ourselves acquainted with every religious fact within our reach in Catholic Europe. Although obstacles arose, everything seemed to finally arrange itself in accordance with our plans.

At the time that we arrived in Cologne it was late in August, and we had before us that equinoctial month of September, during which no landsman wishes to be on the sea. In that month, which this consideration impelled us to still spend in Europe, we would find ample time to make our application, and, if successful, to visit Bois d'Haine.

We left Cologne the afternoon of September 2d, the anniversary of the battle of Sedan— that victory of Prussia, which gave her that terrible and unfortunate predominance in European political circles. European Protestantism and European infidelity have learned from the Catholic Church many an important lesson, and among them the necessity of a joyful repose— that necessity familiarly expressed by the time-worn proverb, " All work and no play makes Jack a dull boy." While laying the cornerstone of their schemes for supplanting Christianity, the infidel governments arrange the practical lessons which they have learned from the Catholic Church according to the rules of their pagan philosophy. Wishing, as they do, to win the people, they are too prudent to reduce them to a decorous rest taken every seventh day, for they know that thus the task of alienating the hearts of the people from the doctrines of the Church would be increased two-fold. Knowing this, they institute political festivals, which they intend shall eventually supercede the holy days of religion. Skilfully as they may mix their pill, they are omitting the important ingredient, for which they substitute a virulent poison. Religious instruction, and, above all, lifting the heart to God in prayer, renders, what would be otherwise a waste of that precious time given to us by God, not to amass wealth, but to work out our salvation, a most beneficial lightening of the load of earning one's daily bread. Political exultation, political rancor beget nothing save drunken frolics, and what is far worse, envy, hatred, and covetousness are exalted into virtues when exercised on a nation whom a government is pleased to style " the enemy."

Such were the reflections that filled our minds as we saw church and town hall alike flaunting the black, white and red of the new German Empire, and the very suggestive black and white banner of Prussia with its vulture-like eagle. From the ancient Cathedral streamed the same emblems of triumph, while hour after hour the vaulted roof re-echoed the one loud, sorrowful appeal, "Let us pray for our imprisoned archbishop."

And yet, as if in mockery of that cry of distress, the city council had decreed that the term "government buildings" should include the churches, and that they, too, must join in the external triumph over the beginning of the downfall of Christianity in the German Empire under the title of the "Deliverance of 1870."

We watched the city fade from our vision as the train bore us westward, nearer towards one of the many acceptable sacrifices of expiation for these scenes of impiety, until the lofty towers and the waving flags were no longer discernible, and we then thought that we had left this exhibition of triumph, but each village through which we passed, each station at which the train halted, repeated the same scene of fluttering canvas and festive garland. At Aix-la-Chapelle the decorations were as numerous and extensive as those of Cologne. Charlemagne's last resting place joined in rejoicing at the defeat of France.

Late in the afternoon the train arrived at Verviers, and, as the railway official opened the door of the coupé, he informed us that all must leave the train. Were we at the Belgian frontier, we inquired. The official replied in the affirmative. But there had been no need to ask the question; not only were the posts at the switches and those holding the signal lights no longer painted in funereal black and white; not only did the officials in the railway station wear a uniform which we had never before seen, but the buildings had no festive decorations, and the general work-a-day plainness told us that we were now in a country that did not keep the humiliations of France in perpetual, triumphant remembrance.

Passports are no longer subject to scrutiny on European frontiers, excepting, of course, in time of war, and it would be agreeable to tourists if the custom of examining private luggage had also fallen into disuse; but Switzerland is the only country that has as yet defined the difference between a merchant and a tourist. The custom-house at Verviers is, however, admirable for the politeness and discretion of its officials, and it will be long remembered by us on that account. We were detained but a moment, and then we were permitted to pass through to the platform, alongside of which lay the train about to depart for Brussels. As this train would not leave for nearly half an hour, we did not enter it immediately, preferring to walk to and fro and observe our new surroundings. The majority of the passengers spoke French, the coupés reserved for ladies traveling alone were marked "Dames," the prohibitions to smoke or to walk on the tracks were written in French, and, in fact, we might have imagined ourselves in France, had not the uniform of the railway officials differed from that of France, and had we not occasionally passed groups of chattering women, or loquacious farmers, rattling off sentence after sentence of Walloon, or slowly enunciating that curious travesty of German, Flemish.

At the appointed time we took our places in the Brussels train, and soon we were borne rapidly still further westward, through neat villages, and over charming rural districts. We were now in a country through which we had never before traveled, and we noted every particular with great interest. Everywhere we saw the same neat cottages, the same well-kept farms, and we realized that we were in one of those little kingdoms too small ever to dream of ruling the world's destinies; where the government, instead of pondering over schemes of glory, thought only of the welfare of its subjects; in a land under the control of that "paternal legislation" so often sneered at by those who do not trouble themselves to make an honest inquiry into the results of its policy. Even when passing through mining districts, we saw no evidence of that combination of extraordinary individual wealth with extreme poverty of the working classes, that painful difference so often seen in regions where the underground resources form the staple products. There were no traces of pauperism, for every class there were substantial dwellings, suitable to the rank of each. Nowhere did we see miserable shanties contrasting with elegant palaces. We were still busy remarking this and admiring the picturesque cliffs of the valley of the Vesdre, when nightfall prevented further observation.

The train rushed rapidly down an inclined plane and halted before a wide semi-circle of light—all that we saw of the ancient city of Liege, so familiar to us from childhood from appearing so frequently on the pages of that charming collection of tales known as the "Legends of the Seven Capital Sins."

In a few moments the train resumed its onward course, and leaving the gas-lit streets of Liege far behind, halted again, this time at that venerable scholastic town, Louvain. Here we alighted, having filled the measure of our usual "day's journey." It was nine o'clock in the evening, the street lamps were all burning, and the railway station but a few rods distant from the town, so, glancing at the signs of the hotels in sight, we directed our steps towards the hotel of the New World, which our guide-book recommended as being well adapted to persons of moderate requirements, and as also being moderate in its charges. We were acting, for the time being, on the no-baggage principle; so, carrying our light luggage ourselves, we arrived at the door of the hotel, without either guide or porter to thrust himself between us and the smiling landlady.

We were now to see a Belgian inn—an experience new to us, and we were all, in a tired way, eager enough to compare it with the many inns of the many nations with whom we had come in contact. We were led through two dining-rooms, each with a bare, deal floor, well scrubbed and well sanded, and up two flights of spotlessly clean wooden stairs, every bit of whose cleanliness was necessary as atonement for their excessive steepness. In the second floor we found two bed-rooms, utterly destitute of carpets, or of any of the so-called comforts of civilization; but the floor was clean, the bed linen spotless, the window curtains were all that the most fastidious neatness could desire, and the rooms actually contained all that is necessary for the repose of the wearied traveler. In the second floor the landlady showed us her best bed-room, the pride and glory of her hotel. Curtains, as we learned from after experience, form an indispensable part of a Belgian bed. In this bed-room they were very elaborate, as were also the window curtains; the quilt was of some Flanders manufacture, and a crocheted tidy covered the green cloth on the centre table. A home-made rug of woolen patch-work lay beside the bed, and a similar one was placed before the black mohair sofa, otherwise the room was without carpeting. Truly, the landlady had made a grievous error when she gave her hotel the name of the "New World," for there was not a sign of New World extravagance or New World luxury; it was rather the Old World, with its practical common sense and its healthful simplicity, the heirlooms inherited from ages of Christian self-denial and abstinence.

We descended the stairway, a type *par excellence* of those which we afterwards learned to designate as "those dreadful Belgian staircases," into the smaller of the two dining-rooms. We were travelers of too great experience to entertain any fears concerning the respectability of our lodgings, for we had long since learned that part of the tyranny of the Old World takes the form of obliging every public house to be as respectable as it professes to be. Had we had any doubts on the subject they would have been silenced by the sight of a priest and two seminarians, travelers like ourselves, taking their simple evening repast, which they concluded by the long prayers for the living and the dead, which characterize the German thanksgiving after meals. As we were very tired, we took a very light supper, and returning to our rooms, we were soon oblivious of all facts regarding furniture of any kind, either plain or handsome.

There is much in Lourain to interest the lover of mediæval art, but we had not the time to visit its old monuments, we were far too anxious to reach Tournay. So, at ten o'clock the next morning, after having despatched a letter to a clerical friend in Rome to beg for a recommendation to the Bishop of Tournay, we took leave of our New World landlady, whose bill did not amount to $2—supper, lodgings, and breakfast, and we might add cleanliness, all included, and this before panic prices were thought of.

We once heard a German gentleman, the superintendent of a large government lumber yard in eastern Bavaria, express himself very drolly, though at the same time very logically, in regard to extravagant travel. To a German, the first-class railway coaches are simply the English and American department of a train; his highest dream of railway luxury is the second class, and our acquaintance made that his standard of comparison.

"I never travel second class," said he "third is good enough for me. It is true that the seats are simply varnished wood, while in the second class one would find very nice upholstery, but even after a man has paid for his ticket that upholstery doesn't belong to him, it is the property of the State Railway. If, every time I traveled in the second class, I might carry home a nicely cushioned arm-chair, then, bravo! I'd always travel in that manner."

And so it is with hotels: if, every time one went to the luxurious homes of fashionable travel, one might carry home some rare carved or gilded wood-work, or some carpet of fine texture, then it would be more excusable to seek scenes of that splendor which does not exist in the majority of private dwellings. Dear reader, cleanliness in your surroundings is the only real requirement of civilized travel. Are you way-worn and weary? You will sleep as soundly in a room whose floor is bare as if it were covered with the richest Axminster. Are you anxious and restless? The dreary hours will revolve as sleeplessly in an apartment crowded with elegant uselessnesses, as sleeplessly as in a simple room containing only the needful furniture. To follow closely the logic of our German friend, those who observe simplicity in their habits of travel will more probably return home, laden with souvenirs of their journeys, than those who exhaust their purses on the temporary enjoyment of a splendor, which, perhaps, does not exist in their own houses. If your friends return from abroad, bringing with them a thousand and one little memorials, do not consider each one as a period in the numeration which the reading of their income would involve; more probably, if these memorials are of a religious nature, they mark some era of self-denial.

Soon after parting from our landlady, we were seated in a Brussels train; this time the holders of tickets for Tournay. In less than an hour and a half we alighted at Brussels, to wait at least two hours and a half for a train that would take us to our journey's end. This long connection reminded us much of our own country, and it renewed an idea which five years abroad had nearly obliterated from our minds; for, in general, European railway connections are prompt and sure. We have, it is true, our vast lengths of railway, connecting great commercial centres, and which transport us over towns and villages as if these last were but the waves of the ocean, but those who have strayed away from these great thoroughfares into the region of less frequented travel, can testify to the tedium of waiting for the train which takes its own time to arrive.

America holds itself forth to the world as the country of railways, and many who ought to be better informed, have a vague idea that European countries are comparatively destitute of that method of locomotion. Belgium has more railways, in proportion to her area, than any other country of Europe, but her neighbors are not so far outdone by this little kingdom as to render her no fair example of the state of railway communication in Europe. The area of Belgium is 11,363 square miles, and the aggregate length of her railways amounted, in 1874, to 1,960 miles. If we reckoned the number and usefulness of our railways by our shocking disasters, we might well think we excelled in every department of this method of travel. We must be always willing to be just to others, even if that justice implies a condemnation of ourselves, and it is only just to say that the ever-watchful governments of the Continent manage to regulate even steam, and to rob it of its explosiveness by the number of rules imposed upon those intrusted with its care. To their old-fashioned eyes, success is no criterion of prudence. Whether the train executes a foolhardy feat without a hair's breadth of injury being done to the freight of human life, or whether it hurls its cargo of souls into eternity, the crime of imprudence is considered equally heinous, and every railway employee is careful to avoid that which, even if successful, will cause him to lose his means of livelihood.

As soon as we had recovered from the dizziness naturally felt on descending from a train, we decided to leave our traveling bags on deposit at the railway station, and then spend our time in rambling about the streets of this Paris in miniature, until the hour of the departure of the Tournay train. We tried to direct our steps towards the famous Cathedral of St. Gudule; but, although it is so conspicuous an object when Brussels is seen at a distance, we failed, amid threading the labyrinth of streets, to see its lofty spires. We did, however, enter one church, which was dedicated to St. John the Baptist, just in time to hear one of those late Masses, so severely criticized by American Catholics. We never did belong to that school of piety (?) and too often have we thus felt the benefit of this kind arrangement to have much patience with such critics. After Mass we employed our remaining spare moments in examining the different altars of this church, and in comparing the incentives to devotion thereon displayed with those of the same class in other countries, and we remarked that the stern realistic representations of Germany were here invested with the expensive magnificence of France.

We returned to the station, reclaimed our luggage, and, taking our places in the train, we were borne still further westward. For several hours we shared the ladies' coupé with a woman of the class that wears a plain, white cap, very much like our widow's cap, instead of bonnets. In both Belgium and France the women of the middle and lower classes rarely ape the fashions of ladies of rank, and, in fact, they would be ashamed to exchange their plain, black cashmere dresses and their neat, white caps, which are often trimmed with beautiful lace, for the garb of a social position which they do not possess. They understand too well that, under the law of God, honest labor has a respectable rank, and that the true way "to raise themselves" is to honor the station of life in which they have been placed by Divine Providence, by becoming and remaining steady, faithful, honest servants. The French and Belgian maids would scorn to dress themselves like their mistresses; they feel that their own costume is equally honorable, and they have not the least desire to be confounded with those flippant characters, who, under the pretence of lawful, laudable ambition, seek to place themselves in situations where they may indulge in vanity and indolence.

The plain black dress and the simple cap— the slavish badges of servitude, as some might term them—did not prevent this young woman from being well-informed on all important local items, and in the course of conversation she displayed a keen judgment, rarely possessed by those who are occupied with the exasperating whims of partially gratified envy.

We did not resent the friendly remarks uttered by her from time to time as impertinent familiarity, for we understood perfectly that where the boundary lines between classes are clearly marked, there is no need to observe that unchristian rule of never conversing with those beneath you, save on matters of duty and necessity. We learned from her that one of the priests of her village had been to Bois d'Haine, and had been permitted to see some part of the weekly miracle; and that afterward, when he returned, he testified to his congregation that it was far more wonderful than could be imagined. She herself had also been to Bois d'Haine, but she failed to gain admittance to the Lateau cottage; she had knocked at the door, and for a long time she received no response; finally, one of Louise's sisters deigned to come out and speak to her. The maid in vain entreated to speak with Louise, and even produced as peace-offerings some pretty prayer-book pictures, which Louise's sister took—steadily refusing, however, to allow the maid to satisfy her pious curiosity.

"Why do you want to see her?" said she; "she is a peasant girl like any other peasant girl, just like yourself. Look at me, if you want to see her; I resemble her very much."

"They tell me," said the maid to us, "that I should have written long before, to announce myself. Who knows?"

"Was it generally believed in Belgium?" we inquired.

"Believed! Oh, yes; everyone in the whole country knows that Louise Lateau suffers every Friday. The infidel journals say that it is a medical secret, of which the priests make use to deceive the people—but who can know how to do a thing like that?"

As she said that, her gray eyes shone with intense amusement at this absurd form of incredulity.

"Why did her sister treat you so brusquely?" we asked.

"Oh, well: they are a simple peasant family, never accustomed to see anyone save their own neighbors, who, like themselves, lead a poor, retired life; now, this publicity they find very disagreeable, and, if they had their own way, no stranger would ever enter their door."

III.

THE morning had threatened rain, and the dripping clouds were fulfilling every portion of the menace, when, at the close of the afternoon, we alighted at Tournay, the ancient Civitas Nerviorum—the first capital of the Merovingian dynasty. Our minds were far away from either its ancient splendor, or its modern interest; we thought only of our lodgings, which, fortunately, we found not far from the railway station in the modest Hotel Bellevue, which was a pretty faithful copy of our resting place at Louvain. Let it not, however, be supposed that Belgium is "so far behind the age" as not to possess any magnificent hotels, for these also exist in all her cities, and, like those of the other parts of the Continent, they sport the very suggestive titles of d'Angleterre and d'Amérique, showing thereby whom they expect for their guests. The natives, and the genuine traveler who comes for the sake of either art or religion, are very careful to avoid those scenes of fashion and flirtation, and to choose the more simple inns for their places of repose.

For the present we had nothing to do, save to rest ourselves and to visit the fine old churches, until the arrival of the letter from Rome. When speaking on the subject with one of the Redemptorist Fathers, the one who then fulfilled the office of "pro Anglica" in Tournay, we were advised by him to make our application immediately. "Others are permitted to witness the miracle," said he, "and why not you? Don't wait for that letter from Rome; go and see our Bishop—he is very amiable, very affable, and besides, he has been a missionary in your country. 'Speaks English!' of course he does. Why, he was pastor of a church in Detroit for many years."

In accordance with this advice, we presented

ourselves at the door of the episcopal palace, where the porter—unlike the one at Spires—received us very politely, telling us that the Bishop's reception hours were in the morning, when, he did not doubt, Mgr. Dumont would be pleased to see persons from the country where he had spent so many years of missionary life.

We did come at the hour indicated, and were ushered into a spacious reception-room, whose lofty proportions were truly palatial. The furniture was extremely simple, being confined to a narrow strip of hemp-carpeting extending across the middle of the floor, the whole length of the room; plain chairs of green morocco upholstery, and portraits of former Bishops of Tournay. While we were contrasting the simplicity of European palaces with the extreme luxury deemed a necessity by the upper classes in America, an ecclesiastic entered and began a series of abrupt questions and answers.

"Were we personally acquainted with Mgr. Dumont?"

"Then why did we wish to see him?"

"No; he had never been pastor in Detroit, but in a village several miles distant from that city."

"Mgr. Dumont was not the owner of Madame Lateau's house—it was not to him that we should apply for permission to enter it."

"Then," said our mother, "it is of Madame Lateau that we must demand permission to witness the miracle?"

He was startled for an instant—as well he might have been—for although we were not then aware of the fact, Madame Lateau had been in her grave several months. He, however, soon replied:

"Go to M. le Curé of Bois d'Haine—it is he whom you must ask."

He left the room as quickly as he had entered it, and he soon returned with a bit of paper, upon which was written the address of the pastor of Bois d'Haine; and at the same time that he explained how very difficult it was to gain admission on account of the number of applicants and the smallness of space, he gave us such ample railway information that it was evidently his chief desire we should leave instantly for Bois d'Haine, so as to be very far away from the Bishop.

That, perhaps, it might give the Bishop pleasure to hear from his former parishioners, many of whom might prove to be our relatives, or our friends, and that these, in turn, might be pleased to receive news of one who had once been their pastor, seemed to be ideas of which the old gentleman had no conception. As we left the reception-room, and the words advising us to compensate ourselves for probable disappointment (by planning a tour in Belgium) had just been uttered by him, we caught a glimpse of a purple robe, and we saw the mild and gentle face which, having remarked at the Cathedral services, had inspired us with the confidence to approach the Bishop.

Mgr. Dumont was coming to the reception-room, but the ecclesiastic stepped forward and said a few works in a low tone. The Bishop looked puzzled, while we, too confused, too perplexed by the cross-questioning through which we had passed, to even remember to ask his blessing, passed down the broad stairway into the court, where the porter gazed wonderingly at us. Evidently, persons from that country where his master had been a missionary, always made longer visits when they entered the episcopal residence of Tournay.

We walked slowly through the Cathedral square, almost disheartened; it was a nearer view of the obstacles which had first loomed on our mental vision at Cologne, and which had assumed a more definite form since our conversation with our traveling companion, the maid. It was evident that the reverend gentleman had no idea that anything save fresh disappointment awaited us at Bois d'Haine, so these obstacles appeared almost insurmountable. Bois d'Haine was proving itself a pilgrimage, for trials and difficulties were shaping a pilgrim's cross.

If we might only be sure that the letter from Rome would come? Friday was fast approaching, and we saw that our chance of admittance would not be until the following week. Feeling that our desires were not based on mere curiosity, we would leave no stone unturned; so, the next day, the same hour found two of us at the door of the episcopal residence, and the puzzled porter, always polite, again informed the Bishop of the presence of the ladies from America. Perhaps, too, the recollection of that mild and gentle countenance gave encouragement to this seemingly audacious step which this time did prove successful.

This time Mgr. Dumont was not intercepted, and he was, as the Redemptorist Father had said, lovely and affable. His parish had been in Detroit itself, and he inquired with great interest concerning his former co-laborers and his former parishioners. When Bois d'Haine was mentioned, a shade passed over his countenance. To him it was evidently a painful subject.

"Formerly," said he, "I did give the permissions to visit Louise; my predecessor did so. But now, that the applications are so very numerous, both Mgr. De Champs and myself have concluded to leave this difficult matter entirely in the hands of the pastor of Bois d'Haine; he seems to understand to arrange all. Now neither myself nor the Archbishop of Mechlin interferes in his decisions.

"I could," added he, after a moment's reflection, "give you a recommendation. I do not promise you that it will be of any avail, but I can give it to you. Do not place too much reliance upon it, for I have ceded all real authority over Louise to the pastor of Bois d'Haine."

Calling one of his secretaries, he bade him write to the pastor of Bois d'Haine, and say that if it were possible to allow these three ladies to be present at the ecstasy of Louise Lateau on Friday, September 18, he, the bishop, would be very much pleased, as he really did desire their admittance.

On being asked why it was so very difficult to witness the miracle; was it really the smallness of space, or did the family seriously object? he exclaimed:

"Object! Why, they just hate it! Louise knows nothing of her visitors, for she is insensible to all her surroundings; but her mother—her sisters! they just hate it! hate it! hate!"

And across his face came an expression that would have been amusement had not the whole subject been to him, as well as to them, a source of annoyance and anxiety. Had God vouchsafed to send this miracle half a century earlier—before steam had brought the nations of the earth so closely together—the prelates of Belgium might have indulged in a holy pride to think that their country had been so blessed; but now, when the world of Thomases is perpetually knocking at their door, this pride is swallowed up by a constant temptation to feel how much more blessed it is to believe when one has not seen.

We remained in Tournay several days after having seen the bishop, because the 18th of September was too far distant to render it necessary to leave immediately after posting the kind recommendation given us by Mgr. Dumont.

Before our departure the letter from Rome arrived, and we were happy to be able to present a proof that his kindness had not been misplaced.

Tournay is essentially a Catholic town, and the march of nineteenth century civilization had not yet deprived it of its primeval Christian simplicity and piety. During our two weeks' stay there we saw much that was of interest to the Catholic traveler, which it would not be especially necessary to relate at present, save by way of illustrating the practices of that school of devotion which meets with the supernatural reward of a standing miracle.

We left Tournay September 15, at noon-day, having taken our tickets for Menage, the railway station on which Bois d'Haine depends. The country was undulating, and, consequently, the grades were very numerous, and over these the rapid motion shook us and jolted us unmercifully. About two o'clock we arrived at Mons, now chiefly important as the centre of a mining district. Here we were to have entered another train, which would take us to Menage, but whether we were one minute too late, or whether we were a whole half hour behind time, we could not discover. Walloon and French were shouted from one angry official to another, and we were made to comprehend that we must wait for a train which was not due for three hours. Five hours later, when we reached Menage, we knew the great discomfort occasioned us by this delay, but at the moment we thought only of the tedium of a railway waiting-room to be endured for three hours.

So tired were we with the rough, sunny ride from Tournay, that we did not have the energy to follow our usual practice of rambling through the streets of a town, where the intervals between trains obliged us to spend some hours. All that we did at Mons was to go to a restaurant to take lunch, which served to strengthen us for the extra fatigue which we were about to undergo.

After three long hours the train did arrive, and it carried us through village after village, where blazing foundry fires told of the vast amount of coal annually taken out of the rich mines of this region. It was nightfall when we arrived in Menage, for it took us a whole afternoon to make a little journey of three hours. However, we spied a number of hotels, and, taking our satchels with us, we directed our steps towards the nearest one, which had a neat and inviting exterior. Inside all was dire confusion—broken walls, freshly plastered; newly-painted woodwork—in fine, all the disorder and discomfort of a house undergoing repairs. We left, and, crossing the railway, proceeded with confidence towards two imposing buildings, calling themselves hotels, sure that at either one we could find accommodation; but both were closed, utterly tenantless. A young girl addressed us; after asking if we were going to Bois d'Haine, she showed us two little inns, in either of which she thought that we could find lodgings. So we recrossed the railway track, and, going first to the one and then to the other, we found that there was no room for us. Night had really come, the stars were distinctly visible; our satchels had grown so heavy, we were so weary, and no place to rest. Never before had we been so situated, and a vague hope arose in our minds that perhaps M. le Curé would grant the wished-for permission, as too many crosses were clustering around Bois d'Haine for it not to be a successful pilgrimage.

We were told that in a village two miles distant there was an excellent inn; but at that hour we could find no one to carry our satchels, and we had neither the courage nor the strength to make any further attempt, so we returned to the place where we first entered, and the active landlady immediately began to clear away some of the rubbish. We took our supper in a dining-room filled with freshly-painted furniture, and, therefore, sickeningly odorous, and our clothes were in constant peril of being stained with paint. The landlady swept and scrubbed two tiny rooms and crowded a few of the bare necessities into them, and then we thought that we could take a peaceful night's rest; but

Menage, although a mere village, is what is termed, in railway language, a junction, and in any country it would be a junction of the first class. If any of the readers of this ever find themselves thus far on a journey to Bois d'Haine let them bear in mind not to spend a night at Menage. When we had half forgotten the day's weariness and discomfort, a flash of lurid light, a heavy rumbling, a shrill whistle, and we were wide awake to aching heads and throbbing temples. All night long every hour brought a repetition of the same thing, and when we arose in the morning it was with a confused idea of signal-lights and head-lights, red lights, white lights, green lights.

After breakfast, two turned their steps in the direction of Bois d'Haine to seek the residence of its pastor. Two only, for by this time we had heard enough of the Curé of Bois d'Haine to fear that if the manner of one offended him it might not be well for the others. One less, one less chance of his detecting anything that he might choose to find disagreeable.

Taking the street that led southward, it was soon found blending with the highway. To the right, amid a thick grove of trees, lay a little hamlet, whose imposing brick church raised its spire high above the tallest trees—Bois d'Haine, as a woman coming along the highway said in reply to inquiries.

"Bois d'Haine, and if the ladies wish to speak to M. le Curé, they should take the path diverging from the broad road, that path leading through the grove."

It was a charming walk; the path wound through grassy fields and under green trees, until it joined another highway. Just beside this highway stood a little brick cottage, with whitewashed walls and a red tiled roof—a tiny miniature of the neat houses abounding in the rural districts of Belgium. Only one story in height, it could not contain more than four rooms and, perhaps, a little garret. Everything bespoke cleanliness; the wooden steps were well scrubbed, the window-panes sparkled, and the coarse muslin curtains were the whitest of white. Together with the marvelous cleanliness—marvelous even in Belgium—there was an air of intense seclusion; the bright green house-door was wide open, perhaps for ventilation, but it only exposed to view a little entry with carefully closed doors; a few geranium plants stood in one window, but the curtains were everywhere so closely drawn as to prevent the gaze of impertinent curiosity; a mysterious air of calm, an atmosphere of holy tranquility, seemed to pervade the spot. The cottage seemed to have a soul—was it Louise's home?

The hamlet of Bois d'Haine was still quite distant, and a railway lay between it and the cottage; but so strong were their feelings, that the two ladies demanded of a child tending cows in the neighboring meadow, whose house might it be?

"It is the house of Louise Lateau, madame; and yonder lies the village of Bois d'Haine," replied the child.

A few minutes more, and the two had arrived in Bois d'Haine. Passing by the schools, one of which is a charitable institution, then still in the process of erection, they found themselves before the village church, an entirely new structure of red brick. Entering the open portals, they were in an interior of true Gothic—a lofty nave, two lateral aisles and a transept, making that cruciform church by which the Catholics of northern Europe mark the distinction between their ecclesiastical architecture and that of the Lutherans. As yet, the interior was but half finished, the temporary altars were evidently those of the former church, and in one end of the transepts hung the Stations of the Via Crucis, rude paintings on wood, half defaced by time and mildew. Yet they were admitted to the new church, for the truly pious do not wish a church to remain destitute of these important adjuncts for trivial reasons, and we should not reject those which are within the means of the congregation, just because they are too small or not suited to our taste. How often does not God, despising the wisdom of the world and choosing that which it calls weak and foolish, work His most beautiful miracles of grace by means of just such rude instruments as these unsightly pictures? Just as unsightly as they were, these Stations were far more precious than the most costly works of modern art, for it is by following the meditations inspired by them that Louise Lateau has arrived on the heights of Calvary.

On the Gospel side of the sanctuary stood a half life-size wooden statue of our Lord as He appeared to Blessed Margaret Mary, a Paris work probably, for we recognized the brilliant, yet delicate coloring of the artists of the Rue St. Sulpice and its neighborhood. Contrary to American ideas of good taste, Continental artists pronounce color, properly applied, an indispensable adjunct to statues of wood or terra-cotta; the facts of nature are carefully copied, and far from resulting in gaudiness, the effect produced is wonderful. A non-Catholic, a modern Sybarite, would have turned the wounds in this statue "painfully revolting," but a Catholic could not fail to find in their startling fidelity to truth, food for devotion and contrition.

The windows in the body of the church are composed of pieces of colored glass, arranged in Arabesque; those behind the high altar are not only larger, but they are the true stained windows, containing the figures of saints. Among these stands conspicuous, St. Francis of Assisi, the glorious chief of those "Angels who bear the likeness of the Living God." Apoc. vii, 2. There is, also, as companion pane to the Sacred Heart of Jesus, Our Lady of the Seven Dolors, there are St. John the Evangelist, and the Prophet Isaias, the Baptism of Our Lord and the Descent from the Cross. Although not executed in the highest style of the art, as produced from the factories of Normandy and Bavaria, these windows would grace many of the most pretentious of our American churches, and they form a suitable adornment to the Church of St. John the Baptist at Bois d'Haine, which, no doubt, its pious founders hope that their descendants will know under the added title of St. Louise. Not far from the new church is a little, long, low building of bricks, well weather-beaten, this is the old church, "which was good enough for us," remarked a workman, as he observed the strangers. Yes, certainly it was good enough for them, in the days when standing under the huge chestnut tree in front of the church door, the groups of laughing peasants had nothing save seed time and harvest to discuss. Perhaps, too, the old church was good enough for Our Lord Himself, since He loves the lowly things of this earth, and when He came to humble peasants it was well enough that they should receive Him in a simple abode, but present circumstances have altered the case. Even were Louise to dwell in entire seclusion, never permitting anyone to enter her cottage, she would still belong to the Christian world, and it is, therefore, eminently fitting that all Christians should unite in erecting this beautiful thank-offering for the great graces here vouchsafed, not only to the people of Bois d'Haine, not only to Belgium, but to the whole Catholic Church.

Beside the church stands the house of the pastor, and it was at its door that the two ladies would learn the results of Mgr. Dumont's intercession. The door was opened by M. le Curé himself, and they saw a priest apparently forty-five years of age; his countenance wore an expression of continual abstraction, such as one might expect from an ordinary mortal who dwelt continually face to face with the mysteries of Gethsemani and Calvary. His general appearance was more distingué than that of the majority of country pastors, though he seemed to possess their usual simplicity united to an eccentricity all his own. Standing in the doorway, with the door half-closed behind him, his hand on the latch, he scrutinized mother and daughter at his leisure. Yes, he had received that letter from Mgr. Dumont, and he had already sent a reply.

"But we did not expect a reply."

"True enough, and I did not know where precisely to address the letter; well, well, come in."

In spite of his abrupt ways, M. le Curé possesses considerable ease of manner, and assigning chairs to the ladies in his little reception-room, he led the conversation in a great many directions, evidently with a view to discover something of the character of the applicants before committing himself. There were a great many "well, wells" on the part of M. le Curé, and a great many apparently irrelevant questions.

"Had they come from Menage to Bois d'Haine without a guide? Did they always do that way?"

"Did they really enjoy travelling? Oh! what a life of discomfort it must be!"

Although armed with intercession so powerful, the ladies were far too prudent to make any imperious demands, neither did they assume too imploring a manner, as M. le Curé could know their desires without their making use of either extreme. In speaking of the church, one said:

"It is not every village that possesses such a church."

"Madame," replied the pastor, "it is not every village that has Louise Lateau."

His manner and voice as he uttered this

showed that he comprehended the greatness of the favor which had been bestowed on the unpretending hamlet.

"Well, well, there are three of you, if I remember rightly what Monseigneur wrote," said M. le Curé, at last, "well, well, come next Friday to Louise's house at a quarter past two; you may remain until a quarter past three. You are lodging at Menage?"

He readily believed the tale of the previous night's discomfort, for it was always so at Menage.

"In coming here," said he, "you passed Louise's house, I am sure; on your return, continue on the paved highway, pass by her cottage, do not take the field road, and the highway will bring you to Fayt, a village half an hour's walk from here. There you will be far distant from railway sounds, and at the Hotel de la Poste you can rest yourselves until Friday."

By following these directions, Fayt was easily found, and satisfactory arrangements were made at the inn de la Poste. The principal street of Fayt terminates in a highway leading to Menage, and twenty minutes after these arrangements had been made, the one who had remained in Menage learned not only that better lodgings awaited the family elsewhere, but also of the success of the application made to M. Niels, pastor of Bois d'Haine.

The landlady, overwhelmed with surprise to think that we had been successful, where every week witnesses so many failures, did not, in the midst of her astonishment, forget to make a very shrewd bargain for her son, who brought a wheelbarrow to carry our satchels to Fayt.

Here all was agreeable comfort, neatly furnished bed-rooms, and a nice little dining-room, where we could sit and read, or else play on the cottage piano, the property of our landlady's little girl; but we preferred the tranquillity of our own rooms, where we spent the greater part of the time between our meals in reading the various sketches of Louise's life which we had in our possession.

IV.

THE pens of men deeply versed in mystic theology, or skilled in medical science have made the American public acquainted with the out-lines of the remarkable portions of Louise's life; but at the same time carelessly worded items appear from time to time in the journals concerning her present condition, calculated to lead astray the minds of those but slightly conversant with the operations of grace in her regard. Therefore, in order to make an account of our experiences at Bois d'Haine more intelligible to the majority of readers, it will be prefaced by an abridgement of Louise's life down to 1874, drawn from various approved sources, which are confirmed by general report in the vicinity of Bois d'Haine. The illnesses and accidents of her childhood are told, in order to illustrate the fact that when God designs certain persons to fulfil particular missions, His Divine Providence watches over them, protects them, and even rescues them from certain death. In that which relates to the supernatural, the due submission is made to the decrees of Pope Urban VIII, and to the canons of the Holy Catholic Church.

Louise Lateau was born January 30, 1850, of respectable parents, poor peasants. Her father was a workman in one of the numerous foundries of the province of Hainault. His slender pittance barely sufficed to support his family, which consisted of a wife and three daughters, of whom Louise was the youngest. After the birth of Louise, Madame Lateau was a prey to a lingering malady, from which she had not even commenced to recover, when Louise being two months and a half old, Gregoire Lateau was seized by the small-pox, then raging violently in Bois d'Haine; in his case it proved fatal, and to add to the misery of this desolate family, Louise herself was struck by the contagion.

The doctor came but rarely, the neighbors never; for the unfinished cottage, which Gregoire Lateau had just begun to erect, was too far removed from the village of Bois d'Haine for any of its inhabitants to be reminded of this poor family by seeing their dwelling; so Louise and her mother had to depend on the little service that could be rendered by a six year old child, that being then the age of Rosine Lateau, the oldest of the three sisters. In one of the doctor's infrequent visits, he enveloped Louise in a large poultice, in which the poor, neglected infant remained for several days. When it was removed, her body was completely black, and hardly a breath of life remained in her. At last, Divine Providence looked with compassion on this deserted family, and sent to their aid a distant relative, a certain Delalieu, who charged himself with their care, until Madame Lateau was, after years of suffering, completely restored to health, and her daughters were old enough to earn their bread.

By the time that Louise had attained the age of two and a half years, she had entirely recovered from all the effects of the small-pox, not even the scars remaining. At this period she again came in close contact with death: one day, while playing with her sister Rosine in a neighboring meadow, she fell into a deep pit filled with stagnant water. Rosine called her mother, who, though still an invalid, ran with all possible speed to draw her child out of the water; Louise was insensible, and her mother, in her ignorance, actually held her with her head downwards for several minutes, so that she might throw up the ditch-water which she had swallowed. God, however, who seldom allows the ignorant efforts of the poor for self-preservation to be followed by serious results, was pleased to bless this well-meant act, and to restore her child to the good woman.

Louise, as it is often the case with the children of the poor, was employed in guarding cattle. One day in conducting two cows to the meadow, she slipped and fell while passing through a narrow lane, and the cow behind her continuing its heavy gait trampled over the body of the poor child. Save the momentary pain, Louise did not immediately feel the effects of this accident, so with that secretiveness peculiar to childhood, she made no mention of it to her elders. Three weeks later, a frightful illness, the result of internal injuries, revealed the mishap; but contrary to all expectations, she was at length restored to perfect health.

The piety of her childhood, in all things a fair sample of the piety of the children of good Catholics, was especially characterized by cheerfulness in the midst of the misery surrounding her, and by an intense desire to nurse the sick. She made her First Communion at the age of eleven years, and from that time she was for five years a semi-monthly communicant.

At the age of fifteen she followed the example of her elder sisters in becoming a seamstress, and she then worked by the day in the families of the neighboring aristocracy. From this short summary of her childhood, the reader may glean that she had very little time to devote to that which is usually termed self-improvement. Her opportunities of education were but few; the five months of preparation preceding her First Communion comprised the whole of her school life, that being all the time that the poverty of the family allowed her to spare for occupations not lucrative. During that time she was taught to read, and she learned to write a little by observing and imitating those of her schoolmates who were sufficiently advanced to practice penmanship.

In the school of Divine Love she made rapid progress; to nurse the sick, to pray for the conversion of sinners, to make the Way of the Cross, and to meditate on the Passion of Our Lord, these were her favorite recreations. At the age of sixteen she became a weekly communicant, but her laborious life gave her ample employment, and she had no time to indulge in any fanciful devotion, which might induce a state of religious frenzy. In fact, even under the most favorable circumstances, it would be impossible for Flemish nature to develop any thing like frenzy, and Louise is as phlegmatic as only a Flemish maiden can be.

It was at this early age that she distinguished herself by heroic acts of charity, not only prompted by sincere piety, but accompanied by firmness and decision. Who does not remember the cholera of 1866? It made but a brief sojourn on our continent, but it was all too long for many. In Belgium it swept alike through hamlet and city, carrying off whole families, devastating whole districts. The little village of Bois d'Haine was a prey to its most frightful ravages, and an epidemic of unearthly fear was its constant companion. In every case the sick members of a household were instantly deserted by the others, no matter how close might be the ties of relationship. Husbands fled from their dying wives, wives rushed from their plague-stricken husbands, parents abandoned their children, children forsook their parents, and few were the chances of a Christian burial.

In the midst of scenes like this, remarked

one of the biographers of Louise, there are three phases of heroism, three examples of self-forgetfulness, three who vie with one another in courage: the doctor, the priest and the Christian woman. With the doctor it is his calling, his means of livelihood; to the priest it is something more even than a vocation, it is a divine obligation; but when the Christian woman leaves home and safety to nurse the plague-stricken, it is an act which takes its place next to the practice of the evangelical counsels, for it possesses a character of voluntary virtue to which certainly the doctor can lay no claim.

Milan and Florence once saw their prelates passing day and night in administering the last sacraments to those dying of the pest. Bois d'Haine was but a hamlet, its pastor a simple village priest, yet his conduct was worthy of the Church that honors St. Charles Borromeo. Had the villagers remained with their dying ones they might have seen their pastor, by night as well as by day, seeking out the sick, to solace all their woes both temporal and spiritual. Often during these labors he thought of his good Louise; here was an extensive field for her pious exertions, and finally he made an appeal to her courage and charity. She was ready and willing, for it was what she had ardently desired to do; but her mother made very natural objections, to which Louise, always obedient, yielded quietly. Her obedience did not prevent her from having recourse to prayer, and she besought the Almighty to move her mother's heart to grant the required permission; this petition was soon heard, Madame Lateau gave her consent, unasked, to the good work, trusting that Divine Providence would mercifully protect her child from the effects of contagion.

The people of the vicinity still relate with wonder how that girl of sixteen, hardly emerged from childhood, seemed to multiply herself through the village, going from house to house nursing the sick and laying out the dead. The incident below recorded will serve to show how her example finally conquered the dreadful panic, caused the well to forget their cowardly fears, and by paying proper attention to the sick and the dead, to lessen the violence of the pest by diminishing the causes of contagion.

In a certain house, there were three cholera patients, a man and his wife and their daughter. The sons, seized with terror, fled from the house, and none of the neighbors dared to enter the afflicted cottage. That Louise imitated their course of action, the reader will not for one instant imagine. The man died; Louise was the only person present when M. le Curé administered the last Sacraments, and when he went to carry the consolation of the dying elsewhere, she was left alone in the house. The woman died the same day, and the sons, trembling with fear, came to take their dying sister away from the village, but they did not offer to see to the interment of their parents. Louise did not desert the dead any more than she had the living, she proceeded to lay out the two corpses that were already impregnating the house with infectious odors, and as she was not strong enough to place them in their coffins, she called to her assistance her sister Adeline. These two girls, whose size would be almost dwarfish were not their tiny figures so well proportioned, succeeded not only in placing the bodies in their coffins, but also in dragging them some distance from the house in the direction of the cemetery. The people of Bois d'Haine could no longer resist this brilliant example, and persons ran in all directions to assist in giving Christian burial to the hitherto neglected pair.

V.

AT the very beginning of the following year Louise was attacked by a lingering illness, the first sickness which she had had since her eighth year, when she was trampled upon by the cow. She suffered from severe pains in her head and from an aggravated sore throat, nevertheless she continued her ordinary occupations until September. On the 18th of September, the eve of the Festival of the Apparition of our Lady of La Salette,* she received the last Sacraments, while her friends began a novena to our Lady of La Salette. She took a few drops of the water of the miraculous fountain, and contrary to all natural expectations, she recovered immediately. This recovery was but a prelude to new pains;

---

*This festival is one "proper" of the dioceses of Belgium.

scarcely had three weeks elapsed when she was again undergoing the most frightful sufferings. Violent neuralgia racked her head, and finally extended itself to the whole of her left side, depriving her of the use of both hand and foot.

Louise not only bore her sufferings with a supernatural patience, but they were evidently the result of a burning desire. That a soul of this description endures sickness not only patiently but lovingly is a mystery to those who are not far advanced in the way of Christian perfection. The trials of the Church, the Majesty of God offended by sin, had long been themes of sadness to her. Had she been one of the many who besought Divine Justice to pour forth the vials of His wrath upon their own unoffending heads and spare His Church? This no one knows, we can only suppose that it must have been.

The year 1868 brought no relief, but rather augmented her torments. The first Friday of that year witnessed the wonderful manner in which God has chosen to make her an atoning victim for you and for me. It was night, but Louise was sleepless, as all who have experienced the horrors of neuralgia can well believe, how her mind was occupied any Christian can surmise. Suddenly a flash of spiritual light penetrated her soul, filling it first with delight and afterwards with sadness, a sadness even unto death. This sadness became pain when communicated to the body, and Louise began to feel the first sensation of the Stigmata. In her entire ignorance of this miracle she did not pay much attention, only recollecting the events of this night, when the Stigmata finally became visible.

Meanwhile a painful abscess made its appearance in the armpit. The remedies applied by the physician brought no relief whatever, one alarming symptom succeeded the other, and at last, on Passion Sunday, a violent hemorrhage threatened to put an end to her life. Two weeks later, she received the last Sacraments, and while making her act of thanksgiving, she was inspired to ask God for life and health.

She asked for health, that she might be able to assist her mother; and for life, that by fresh sufferings she might become more worthy of the promises of Christ.

The moment that Louise had finished her prayer, she knew that it had been heard; at the same time she learned that she was destined to great suffering, but of what nature she did not know. She repeatedly foretold to her family and to M. le Curé that on the 21st of April she would present herself at the village church to receive Holy Communion. They did not place much faith in her prediction, especially when the eve of that day found her still feeble, still confined to her bed; but to their surprise, on the morning of the 21st she arose and dressing herself without aid she was soon ready to go to the church, which she entered at 7 A. M. in full health. Her words had been spread through the village where she was so well known, and the congregation had assembled, as they themselves said, to see the miracle.

For this day and the two succeeding ones no

person in Bois d'Haine thought of the Stigmata, least of all, Louise, who, although a member of the Third Order of St. Francis, was totally ignorant of this saint having received the Five Wounds of our Lord. Why a girl of her extreme piety had thus been ignorant of this important fact it is difficult to divine. Madame Lateau, an honest, straightforward Christian woman, also never knew that the frequent repetition of this miracle was one of the glories of the Church, until she saw it exemplified in her own family. We can give ample testimony that there has existed among the *laity* of France and Belgium—let the clergy speak for themselves—a class who consider it unnecessary, nay, even harmful, for the world in general to be cognizant of the wonders which God has wrought in His saints. Lives of the saints have been written in which all the supernatural has been omitted!

"The wonders, the miracles," say the authors of those works, "give no food to our devotion, they do not concern us, not furnishing us with any practical example of virtue; let us rather turn to the penances, the good deeds, the maxims."

These penances were often performed in obedience to certain visions, and not without permission from prudent confessors, and what ought to be well considered—in climates very much milder than our own, or, at least, more suitable to those particular forms of a mortified life. Certainly we should admire and respect those penances, but we must bear in mind that we may not emulate them without the express permission of our spiritual directors. The virtues of the saints were those of their particular vocations, they were practised under certain circumstances; for those actions to be virtues in us would, perhaps, require that Divine Providence should surround us with precisely the same conditions. Here, again, we must pay the tribute of respect and admiration, but our confessor will tell us how far we may imitate them. Their maxims were uttered in the midst of other social customs, in another age, perhaps in another nation—all of which, most probably, it would be necessary to recall in order to comprehend the real nature of the advice. For example, that "much mis-quoted saint," as some one has called St. Francis de Sales, said to nations dwelling in the midst of bare stone floors, and hard wooden furniture, and praying in cold marble churches, "put yourselves at your ease while you pray." Did he ever suppose that this maxim uttered in favor of the plain oaken priedieux, or the simple wooden bench of a European church would ever be applied to luxurious cushions in pews and on kneeling benches? Just one more example of the manner in which saintly counsel can be misconstrued. More than two hundred years ago, before infidelity had attained its present power, before incredulity had attempted to enter among the children of God, in the retirement of her cloister, in the midst of women aiming at religious perfection, St. Jane Frances told her daughters not to waste the time appointed for the religious reading, by dwelling on visions and miracles. Doubtless, she saw that in them was being developed a love of the marvellous, incompatible with the spirit of their vocation, and derogatory to the dignity of the supernatural; but when we repeat her advice, we should remember that she added, "*leave them for those who need them.*" And in this age of atheism who does not need them?

Often, while we think in many other matters that we are following the example of the saints, we are doing things almost cruel, we are uttering cold, harsh words, instead of consoling, Christ-like comfort; but there is something in the divine light shed by the supernatural which wonderfully illumines the virtues of the saints, and shows more clearly to our spiritual vision wherein we may imitate them. Humility is a powerful instructor, and she is most readily found by viewing what God has revealed of His exceeding great glory; thus we see how very far we are from being at the summit of perfection. Do we then feel a disturbance in our minds, it is not faith that is lessened, it is pride that is wounded.

No food for devotion in meditating properly

on these miracles! Ah, such little comprehend that true devotion consists in glorifying the wonderful works of God, and not in surrounding oneself with a stern virtue whose foundation lies in pride. St. Jane Frances did not wish to deter her spiritual children from giving credence to the miraculous; she merely desired them not to distract themselves with details, but to hasten and contemplate in their existence the glimpses of that glory whose infinite beauty furnishes the Seraphim with an eternity of love and thanksgiving!

"We are not seraphs," would these authors reply, "and the knowledge that these wonders exist is really injurious to the faith of the multitude."

The religious history of the eighteen centuries, which have elapsed since Christ founded His Church, forms a fitting supplement to the Sacred Scriptures, a continuation of the New Testament, which is ours to be taught us, to be explained to us; ours as fully as any portion of the history of Divine action, from the creation of the world until the establishment of Christianity. Therefore, the faith which knows that God had an eternity of existence before he called the universe into life, that is not dazzled by the lightenings of Sinai, that is not scandalized by the Manger and the Cross, and that kneels believing before the Blessed Sacrament, might well be trusted with the knowledge of any miracle however wonderful, of any vision however exalted.

Denial and concealment are no real attributes of the Catholic Church. Italian theologians tell us that Truth is one and immutable, and that her advocates must declare her openly, fearlessly; if apparently she seem against their dogma they must still declare her, and if they stand by her faithfully she will in turn vindicate them. Acting on this principle, they make their people sharers in the knowledge of the lives of their holy ones, and every miracle, every wonder is well-known among the masses. Results speak loudly in favor of their system, for nowhere does implicit faith exist more fully than it does in Italy, not even among those dwelling in the shadow of Calvary or on the olive-clad hills of Bethlehem. Faith reigns supreme, and no heresy of these times can trace its origin to that land, the centre of living Christianity.

Yet other Christian nations often have too little confidence in Italy, and many of the household echo the voice of anti-Catholicism, in saying that " religion is preferable and purer where less mingled with superstition." We are very proud of our title Roman, but we often refuse to place any reliance on the immediate surroundings of the Eternal City. Unfortunately, Italy has had her revolutions; but in spite of the Reign of Terror and the Commune, not to speak of intervening riots, self-styled revolutions, Catholic France, in spite of Calvanism, Jansenism and Gallicanism, still retains, has not lost the respect of the Christian world. Why should we pour forth our righteous indignation indiscriminately upon all Italians, when in France we are able to make the distinction between the desperate outlaw and the peaceful citizen, between the Red Republican and the Legitimist? Why should we close our eyes to the thousands who frequent Loretto, while we gaze so lovingly on the groups around Notre Dame de Lourdes and Notre Dame de la Salette? Yet it is so, and the teachings of any other Catholic country are too often considered preferable to the voice of Italy; nay, the circumstance of something being customary there, or that it happened to an Italian, would cause that practice or that event to be eyed with disfavor by many calling themselves sincere Catholics.

These observations, while intended to throw some light upon the manner in which we may render miraculous events available to our own sanctification, will also explain why Louise Lateau's family did not know of the Stigmata, that brilliant jewel in the common treasury owned by the Communion of Saints. Whether it was unnecessary knowledge, injurious to the faith of Bois d'Haine in general, and harmful to the virtue of the Lateau family in particular, the Almighty Himself took the task of judging.

Friday, April 24th, Louise was again conscious of pain in the five localities of the Stigmata, and a wound made its appearance in her left side; it bled plentifully, but, with her habitual reticence, she mentioned the fact to no one, and the next day the wound was entirely healed. The next Friday blood issued, not only from her side, but also from the upper surface of her feet—again concealing these facts from her family, she, however, made M. le Curé her confidant. The conclusion that he drew he did not dare to admit to himself, much less to Louise, who, obedient to his advice, still preserved silence on the subject. The third Friday the blood flowed profusely, not only from her side and from both surfaces of her feet, but also from her hands—thus rendering further concealment impossible.

M. le Curé advised Louise to apply to the physician at Fayt, who, although a Catholic, actually undertook to cure the Stigmata. One might laugh at so great a folly, were not the five wounds of our Lord too sacred a theme for merriment. Had it been necessary for this physician to be familiar with this "faith-disturbing" miracle? While we ask this question, we cannot deny that his ignorance served a purpose—it helped to establish the reality of the miracle in Louise's case. But there is not from the southern slopes of the Alps to the most remote corner of Sicily—that fair island—which, half occidental, half oriental, rests between the Adriatic and the Mediterranean, one village doctor who would for an instant imagine that these sufferings could come within the range of his medical power. In these latter days, alas! it might be too easy to find those who, to please a silly, an incomprehensible vanity, style themselves "liberals," "free thinkers," "infidels," but whatever opinions the idle lips of such a one might utter, the beautiful legends of infancy would be stored in his heart. He would remember how his mother, or, perhaps, a brother, or a sister scarcely older than himself, had, in the days of a pious, trustful childhood, explained the paintings and statues of St. Francis of Assisi, which, no doubt, occupied prominent places in the churches of his native town. He would also, perhaps, recollect how, when boyhood was just developing into manhood—while life was fresh and beautiful to him, because the shadow of the world's defilement had not as yet clouded the serene purity of his soul—a believing heart and willing feet had borne him over the green Umbrian hills to pray on the spots hallowed by the footsteps of St. Francis. One glance at the bleeding form of the simple peasant maid would have aroused all these holy recollections; one glance would have pierced his very heart, and the words, "God be merciful to me a sinner," would have burst from his lips.

But with the doctor of Fayt it was otherwise. Had he ever heard of any similar miracle? Probably not; and if he had, no doubt it was coupled with the words, "It is not an article of faith, you know."[*] His efforts resulted

---

[*] Were we to confine ourselves to that which we are obliged to believe, we would not advance very far on the way of perfection. With regard to the Stigmata of St. Francis of Assisi, we

in causing poor Louise the most excruciating torments; but the progress of the miracle was uninterrupted—each Friday the five wounds appeared, each Saturday they were completely healed, only a little redness of the skin remaining.

Towards the middle of June, no relief having been obtained, Louise was permitted to give up his treatment. This same physician now declares that he never attempted to cure Louise of the Stigmata; but the fact is too well known in the vicinity for him to deny his egregious mistake. However, he cannot with justice be made an object of ridicule, since he is only the victim of a false system—a system which is loudly demanding admittance into our New World Catholicism.

To use the language of mere science, these weekly recurring wounds in localities, which make them at least a wonderful coincidence,

---

may safely believe in them; for the Church has established a special festival to honor them—*Chiunque negasse le sacrosante istimate di santo Francesco si potrebbe procedere contra di lui siccome contra eretico. Fioretti de S. Francesco Cap. XIII.*

were in Louise's case accompanied by other phenomena not less remarkable. The most conspicuous among them is the state of ecstasy in which her Friday's sufferings terminate—the first traces of this condition made their appearance long before the Stigmata. One day during the summer of 1867, when, while making the Way of the Cross, she was meditating on the third station, Jesus falls for the first time under the weight of the Cross, a flash of spiritual light flooded her mind, increasing her humility, and causing her to reproach herself because she had so little love of God. The state of abstraction caused by this meditation was the first sign of the ecstasies which, afterwards, joined themselves to the miracle of the Stigmata. During the days of convalescence, which succeeded the 15th of April, 1868, those who visited her sick room remarked, that frequently the countenance of Louise was illumined by an expression of radiant happiness, which gave the hard features of the peasant girl a beauty almost angelic; but, if on these occasions her senses failed her, the recall to outer life was so instanstaneous that no one remarked any abstracted manner.

The first decided indication of these ecstasies was a certain absorption in God, which accompanied the weekly apparition of the Stigmata—an absorption which, on the day following, the Feast of Our Lady of Mt. Carmel (the thirteenth Friday of the miracle) was changed into ecstasy. At first, this ecstasy was variable, coming and going every day of the week, every hour of the twenty-four; but in 1874 it was already a long time since it had had a fixed boundary which varied but slightly. This ecstasy was then restricted to Friday, and it began between the hours of 1 and 2 P.M., sometimes later, but never earlier—always terminating between 4 and 5 P.M.

Louise never knows the exact moment that it may arrive; she may be in the act of speaking, in the middle of a sentence; she may be listening to an exhortation; she may be replying to a question, when suddenly the fixed gaze, the radiant face, tell the bystanders that her communication is now with another world.

What is taking place? What is she seeing? Listen to her own words:

"I am seized with an intense, a vivid sense of the presence of God. I see His immensity and my own nothingness, and I know not where to hide myself." [See frontispiece].

This illumination of the mind is immediately followed by a lesser light, by which Louise is made to witness all the scenes of our Lord's Passion from Gethsemani to Calvary. She sees Him in all the stages of the Passion, but she is simply a witness, not a sharer, in the action; and our Lord never notices her. She is insensible to the outer world, but, nevertheless, even during this state of insensibility the voice of ecclesiastical authority, the voice of the Church, can reach her mind. The single word "Louise," uttered by any one of her ecclesiastical superiors, or by a person to whom, even unknown to her, they may have transmitted their authority, will suffice to recall her to herself;

and she replies to the questions which that person may make, although she will relapse into her spiritual slumber as soon as the reply is finished. When she is in this state, present her any object that has been blessed, and she exhibits an instant desire to grasp it; read to her any prayer of the Church, any psalm in any language, and the ecstatic expression will vary according to the words and the sense of the prayer; utter before her the name of any of the celebrated shrines of Our Lady, or of any of the localities where an authentic apparition of the Blessed Virgin has taken place, and a supernatural joy beams forth from every lineament.

VI.

HE services of the physician at Fayt were no longer required, but the matter could not rest thus. Whether these Stigmata, these ecstasies were the results of natural disease, or proceeded from some supernatural cause, some more skilful surgeon must determine. If supernatural, then the Church must apply the subtle tests of theology to discover if they came from the Divine Hand, or if they were not some of the innumerable deceits of the devil.

The clergy, especially the clergy of the North, are very slow to proclaim the reality of a miracle, much slower than the laity; and M. Niels, the pastor of Bois d'Haine, was among the least credulous. Thomas thought it sufficient to behold the Wounds of his Lord; M. Niels, so those who know him best tell us, would not have been content with so slight a proof, and we may be sure that he did not bring the matter before the ecclesiastical authorities until the necessity of so doing became not only apparent but urgent.

The family of Dechamps, of which the Archbishop of Mechlin is a member, possesses a handsome villa near Menage. Here the Archbishop came to enjoy a few weeks of repose during the month of August, 1868, and the result of the interviews that he then had with M. Niels and with Louise was, that Mgr. Ponceau, the Bishop of Tournay, appointed a committee of inquest to investigate the facts of the case.

The religious department of this committee was composed of two learned priests—one a Passionist, the other a Redemptorist. Science was personified by the eminent Dr. Lefebvre, Professor of Medicine at the University of Louvain. Of the medical examination, the learned work of that truly Christian physician is a standing monument. The theological portion is recorded in the written reports presented by the clergy to Mgr. Ponceau—reports which will not be fully published until Louise's death will bring the subject to the direct notice and jurisdiction of Rome.

During the period of this inquest the miraculous course of events continued, and several new circumstances made their appearance. Shortly after the commencement of the inquest, she was subjected to very severe trials, and on Friday, the 18th of September, 1868, one of the priests of the inquest thought that he had discovered in her traces of deception. She received his rather violent reproof with great patience, and the very next Friday the crown of thorns made its appearance, as if to justify the Bride of Christ. Each Friday the bloody diadem became more and more defined—Louise suffered violent pains in her head, as if she were crowned with a burning circle, and blood flowed abundantly from tiny apertures. Ever since then, the effects of the invisible crown have been the inseparable accompaniments of the Stigmata, although they vary—some Fridays only producing pain, without any traces of bleeding.

Notwithstanding all this, the members of the inquest were slow to believe the Divine origin of these facts, and, thus, a year later we find one of the Fathers endeavoring to persuade Louise that these apparent miracles were the work of the Evil One. Out of obedience, Louise tried to believe that such was the case, but her heart was filled with sorrow to think that she was so completely in the power of the devil. One day of the month of August, 1869, after hearing a long argument on this subject, while she was plunged in grief and bewilderment, suddenly she beheld Our Lord standing before her. His countenance wore an expression of intense sadness, and, at the same time, of great compassion. Louise was not in an ecstasy—she saw Our Lord as we see one another, and, for the first time in all her life of visions, she heard His voice speaking to her. He addressed her in these words :

"My daughter, why art thou so discouraged?"

No sooner were these words uttered, than Louise felt her sadness disappear, her doubts vanish—never again to disturb the peace of her soul.

Now, the readers are earnestly requested to pay strict attention to the following seven or eight paragraphs, in order that they may not be led astray in the future by those notices of Louise which speak of her as eating *scarcely anything*. We in this country are so unaccustomed to an accurate recital of the marvelous portions of the lives of holy men and women, that it seems to be impossible for us not to regard certain statements as merely hyperbolical sentences, expressive of the admiration of the narrator for certain extreme practices of self-denial, which, severe though they may be, are yet within the limits of the purely natural.

The nourishment of the peasantry of Europe is extremely simple, and at first the charitably-inclined would be shocked to see the almost entirely vegetable diet upon which they subsist, for it is difficult for classes reared to depend upon meat for the support of physical strength, to believe that a diet in which animal products form so slight a part is really voluntary. Lady Bountiful is frequently astonished to find her kindly-meant efforts in securing to her poor a good supply of meat not rewarded with the amount of gratitude naturally expected by her. Often the boldest among those receiving her kind attentions will, at last, find the courage to beg to receive less meat and more of that same black bread which had aroused so much sympathy. Nevertheless, the peasantry in general have very hearty appetites, and their black bread disappears rapidly when once within their reach. Louise, however, was always an exception to this last; naturally abstemious, she partook but sparingly of any nourishment, even before the beginning of the extraordinary part of her life. After the apparition of the Stigmata, it was impossible for Louise to eat anything on Friday, and, although on other days she ate regularly, still it was only with great effort and out of obedience to her mother.

It was, also, about this period that she began to exhibit that wonderful indifference to heat and cold, which shows that she, being warmed by the fire of Divine Love, is insensible to all variations of temperature.

After the crown of thorns appeared on her forehead, sleep vanished from her eyelids. St. Rose of Lima worked all day, and, with the exception of three hours devoted to sleep, she prayed all night. Louise does not have even these three hours of repose, and, until two years ago, her day spent in household labor was succeeded by a night of prayer or of watching with the sick. Her simple room, so long destitute of any of the appliances of sleep, told us very forcibly how, when chroniclers write that zealous missionaries have journeyed "night and day for weeks," seeking the salvation of souls, that this language is not mere hyperbole, but that these holy men have been by Divine interposition dispensed from the necessity of the refreshment of sleep.

The Feast of the Compassion of Our Lady, March 30th, 1871, was the beginning of her long abstinence, and since then her stomach refuses to accept of any food. Her family and her medical advisers, supported by the authority of her spiritual directors, endeavored to conquer that which they considered an alarming symptom, but these efforts, like the attempts to cure the five wounds, only resulted in torturing poor Louise—her stomach persistently refusing to retain the least particle of food. Now Louise neither sleeps, nor eats, nor drinks; yet, with the exception of Friday, she was, until two years ago, well, strong, and able to work steadily and to advantage, and she was not as much exposed to the inconvenience of occasional, unexpected illness, as many of those who support life under its ordinary conditions, although she was by no means exempt from all the ills to which human existence is liable.

We New World Catholics have, unknown to ourselves in many respects, copied from our immediate surroundings, and one example of this is a so-called devotion to the Sacred Scriptures—a certain respect, whose tenacity does not always resemble that devotion which arouses the cloistered religious of both sexes from their midnight slumbers to chant the praises of the Most High in the same words employed centuries ago by the Chosen People of God, that devotion which causes the cathedrals and convents of the Old World to re-echo almost unceasingly the inspirations of the Royal Psalmist. Our devotion rather consists in obliging our Holy Mother the Church to render a very strict account of herself to our Douay Bible, and when she has done this to *our* satisfaction we are very proud of her, scarcely dreaming of her other countless perfections. For us this habit increases the difficulty of comprehending how Louise can continue to exist under these conditions. In vain, perhaps, would one quote passages in the life of St. Catharine of Sienna, or the Lenten Fasts of that grand model of a faithful wife and a widow indeed, St. Catharine Flisca, or the years of total abstinence from all nourishment—

so prominent in the remarkable life of the Swiss hermit, Blessed Nicholas von der Flüe. The miraculous facts of their lives, although authenticated by Rome, are not scriptural, and we demand not only to know our religion for "our own sanctification and our own salvation," but also in order that we may furnish proofs to those who refuse to believe the Divine origin of the Catholic Church.

In turning the pages of the Old Testament we often read of public fasts, whose completeness and whose duration were certainly supernatural. To quote a case of individual fasting, the prophet Elias, by means of the miraculous loaf given him by the angel, journeyed forty days and forty nights unto the mountain of God. III Kings. xix chap., 8 verse. In speaking of John the Baptist, Our Lord once said: "He came to you neither eating nor drinking." Matt. XI, 18. Our Lord Himself gave us the example of a prolonged fast. Some may say that this was a Divine fast impossible to humanity, but it seems hardly necessary to remind the reader that God's eternal existence being independant of food, fasting is a thing which cannot be affirmed of it. This fast was certainly miraculous, but still it was the human nature of our Lord that fasted, that nature united inseparably to the Godhead, that nature which is sacred, Divine, yet forever human. His reply on this occasion to the first words of temptation are worthy of our profound meditation: " Not by bread alone doth man live, but by every word which proceedeth out of the mouth of God." Matt. IV, 4.

Louise's *sole nourishment for more than six years* has been this Eternal Word uttered before all ages, Our Lord Himself who, in the Blessed Eucharist, is now her daily guest. The Bread of Angels has deigned to prove to us of this generation the extreme truth of those words which so many, even unto this day, find a hard saying, but which are so full of sweetness to the ear of faith: " I am the Bread of Life that cometh down from Heaven." " My flesh is meat indeed." John VI.

The theological inquest lasted more than two

years, and at its close the established order of the apparition of the stigmata was as follows: Thursday night, towards midnight, the wound in her side opened and bled. This bleeding of the side was followed by the opening of the wounds in the hands and feet, which sometimes bled from both surfaces, sometimes from one only. Early in the morning the marks of the crown of thorns made their appearance, and thus at the time at which she received Holy Communion on Friday, the stigmatisation was complete. At that period of her life she was perfectly able to receive in the parish church on other days, and it was only on Fridays that the Holy Communion was brought to her house. By Friday noon all wounds, save those in the hands, began to cease bleeding, and at the hour of ecstasy all traces of the crown of thorns had usually disappeared. This order continued as long as the stigmatization was confined to Friday, if there was any variation, it was so slight as not to be mentioned in an abriged notice.

April 4th, 1873, Louise received a new and

painful wound, the counterpart of that one caused our Lord on His shoulder by the burden of the Cross. Thus she can truly say in the words of St. Paul, "I bear in my body the marks of the Lord Jesus." Galatians VI, 17.

It is hardly necessary to explain here to those who really believe in the Communion of Saints the utility of Louise's sufferings, since they know the nature and use of the contents of the spiritual treasury of the Church—that treasury which is free to all the friends of God. Neither is it necessary to tell them that the penances and sufferings of a Christian are available to eternal welfare both for himself and others, for they well comprehend, without further explanation, that this doctrine, far from being derogatory to the true idea of the Redemption, explains how Our Lord effected the salvation of mankind, by purifying and sanctifying our actions, our sufferings, our prayers, so as to render them acceptable to God. But the true Catholic makes the same question as those outside of the Church : " Why these sufferings ?"—though he awaits a different response—a response which he has already formed in his heart. His mind has already carried him in spirit to all those spots of the Christian world where God's Church is suffering the assaults of the wicked; and when he thinks of all her trials, he wonders that the bright sun can shine upon such scenes of sorrow, and he is surprised that her children can find it in their hearts to rejoice, when that which should be dearer to them than all else beside, is so sorely afflicted, and then he is almost certain that Louise is one of the grand atoning victims for the wrong-doings of this century.

Yes, she is evidently one of that glorious company of whom our Holy Father Pius IX was the chief. When will God have mercy on us, and for their sakes hear our prayers? Who knows? perhaps He heeds them all the while, and tempers to our enduring the fierce storm that is raging, and perhaps for their sakes these days will be shortened.

The date of the occupation of Rome by the

Piedmontese troops, September 20, 1870, was one memorable to Louise, for during that time, when the anti-Christian world was uniting in one wild cry of exultation, she was undergoing the most frightful suffering, and concentrating and personifying the grief of all faithful Catholics.

During the following Holy Week, that of 1871, the Jewish and infidel circles of Paris and Rome were engaged in a rivalry of blasphemous conduct. The leaders of the Commune were, if possible, excelling in iniquity Robespierre and his comrades, and at Rome, at a grand infidel banquet given on Good Friday, a crucifix was placed on the table to receive the insults of the riotous guests. Louise—neither she nor her directors knew of the frightful events of the day, save through her excessive sufferings. Would she survive them? Her state of speechless torture gave them cause to fear that she might fall beneath the weight of her cross, never to rise again.

As we found Louise, we describe her, the

chief events of her life up to the 18th of September, 1874, are all narrated. It is our testimony that is here given, our declaration of what we saw and what we learned while at Bois d'Haine; let those who have seen her within the last two years tell us about her present state of continual stigmatization. It does not come within the scope of a work addressed solely to Catholics to produce the medical proofs contained in the works of Dr. Lefebvre. To those who require these proofs and details, let it be said they exist, and that Berlin philosophy, that dying gasp of Teutonic paganism, which this country is pleased to invest with the laurels stolen from true knowledge, has been repeatedly challenged to give them a logical refutation, and its only reply has been—sneers and gibes, the last refuge of sophistry.

In addition to Dr. Lefebvre, physicians of every country, of every school, of every shade of belief or disbelief, were allowed, and are still permitted, all freedom to inquire into the phenomena presented by Louise's condition. This strict public inquiry makes the Catholic reader blush for the century in which we live; the century that shows us how Herod would have treated the miracles that Christ withheld from him and his mocking courtiers. Thomas, when told by his risen Master to put his finger in the place of the nails, only responded by the exclamation, "My Lord and my God!" The science of the nineteenth century has shown us that it would have joyfully accepted the invitation, and that its enquiring, curious finger would, like the spear, have found its way to the very Heart of Our Lord. Are we Catholics fallen so low in the scale of faith that, in order to believe a miracle, we must be informed concerning that from which our respect for Christian virginity should teach us to restrain our curiosity? If such is the case, how that fact ought to humiliate us.

In reading the details of these medical inquests, which are scattered through nearly all the accounts of Louise's life, the true Catholic will sigh for those ages of faith when, in such cases, learned physicians transmitted their documents to the ecclesiastical authorities alone; when all that a believing laity required to know of the results of their investigations was: *Non est in naturâ.*

"*Non est in naturâ,*" but does it come from God? As far as human wisdom can go it has been ascertained with tolerable surety that all that the Evil One does in this case is to persecute Louise with the same style of attentions with which he usually favors the especial friends of God. Before sleep ceased to be a necessity to her, he often aroused her from profound, healthful slumbers to throw her violently on the floor, or to strangle her, or else to present horrible pictures to her mind, or often to alarm her with hideous noises—in fact, to exhibit his complete repertory of annoyances, with which the life of the Curé d'Ars has made the Catholic public of to-day familiar, showing us that it is not only Job's steadfast faith and virtue that could provoke his malice.

The Church has one infallible test of true spirituality—implicit obedience. This test has been repeatedly tried on Louise, and there is but one last proof needed, and that is final perseverance, for which we must wait until death brings the crown of victory. Catholics ought to know, if they do not, that a state of perfection cannot exist on earth. Of this subject the See of Rome spoke centuries ago, in condemning the errors of Origen : " Holy people are only approximately perfect, at any moment rude temptations may shake the very foundations of their soul, and were it not for the intervening grace of God, who can answer for the consequence ?" As the matter now stands the pious faithful are allowed to exercise that glorious privilege of Christianity—belief; allowed to respond, as former ages did, to the *non est in naturâ* that proclaimed a miracle. It is not in nature, let us give thanks to God for His great glory.

VII.

IN strength and deliberate movement the Flemish brain is a fitting counterpart of the proverbial sturdiness of the Flemish physical constitution. It lingers around profound science with an intensity of thought wearisome to minds less Teutonic in frame, and it delights in weighty metaphysical problems. A proposition once proved, it is not satisfied, but it dwells anew on each ramification of argument, and adds proof on proof—the more abstruse the better—until more volatile intellects have either lost sight of the primary subject, or have but a dim and perplexed idea thereof. Such, at least, was the impression made on us by the works concerning Louise Lateau, with which we had provided ourselves before coming to Bois d'Haine, and it was an impression strengthened by the recollection of a little exhortation which we had heard in the Church of the Redemptorists in Tournay. The congregation, composed of men, women and children of every age and condition, was advised to take as a subject of meditation God's eternal existence, before all ages, before all creation. We knew that to minds like Faber's this is a most restful idea, but no simile of lofty mountain peak, limitless plain or shoreless ocean, had ever done more than to oppress our minds with the immensity of an idea which they were too finite to contain, and we had always sought refuge in the simple phraseology of our little catechism, " God always was and always will be," and so had dismissed the thought, acknowledging ourselves too little and too weak to soar near the incomprehensible mysteries of the Holy Trinity. The Belgian congregation listened calmly to this advice, and doubtless many followed it; and we thought what well-balanced minds these people must have! This was not the only impression produced on us, we gained by this a still clearer idea of the blessing of being born in a Catholic land and of generations of Catholicism. Among us the power of dwelling in meditation on these great truths of revelation is only the prerogative of higher holiness, but here it seemed to be the birthright of the ordinary Christian. Such is the inheritance of a nation which has enjoyed the frequent reception of the Sacraments for centuries.

Our bodies were cramped and wearied with the trying journey of the preceding day, and our brains were thoroughly fatigued by our endeavors to disentangle the miraculous from the medical and the metaphysical; so we closed our books, and, taking our out-door wraps, we sallied forth to pay that, in Europe, commonplace act of devotion—a visit to the Blessed Sacrament. Motion would be physical refreshment, and a little quiet prayer would rest the mind. We found the church in Fayt locked—no great misfortune, we thought, for M. Niels had told us that the church of Bois d'Haine was always open, and we were delighted to extend our walk in that direction, that being the only bit of road resembling a pleasant promenade in the neighborhood. Although so many degrees further north than our own latitude, we found the sunny air as bland and invigorating as on one of our own bright September afternoons; and we were enjoying our freedom from the thraldom of town life, and forgetting all the minute medical proof, almost as trying to the nerves as the accurate annals of a dissecting-room, all the fine distinctions between spiritual slumber and genuine ecstasy, when we found ourselves in the midst of a little adventure, which confirmed the idea which we had naturally formed of Louise's sisters from the account given us by the maid with whom we had traveled on our way to Tournay.

On our return from church, as we drew near to the house of Louise Lateau, we met a woman, dressed in the usual garb of the working classes. She viewed us with considerable displeasure visible in her countenance, and, turning from the highway, she ran rapidly up the steps of the cottage, and, entering, she slammed the green door with a vehemence that would have daunted the boldest heart, and have prevented the most audacious from intruding. Having no intention of going where we had not been invited, we merely noted her conduct as tallying with the general reputation of the Lateau family. We afterwards related the incident to our landlady, who required of us a description of the person whom we had seen.

"It is Rosine Lateau, Mademoiselle," said she; "she and Adeline have that peculiar manner of closing the door, when they imagine that anyone wishes to enter their house, and that is whenever they see anyone on the public highway leading from Fayt to Bois d'Haine; and, perhaps, you will find that M. Niels himself can close that door, when necessary, with a touch of that same manner."

Pausing a moment from her labors, our landlady seated herself by the piano, and repeated her already twice-told tale of her intense desire to witness the miracle and of M. le Curé's steady refusal. This narrative invariably concluded with a dissertation on the disagreeable points of Madame Lateau's character, whose death our hostess considered a blessing to all who visit Louise. If we may trust all that is told in the neighborhood of Bois d'Haine, Madame Lateau and her two older daughters did not, to use a familiar expression, put their best foot forward on Friday. Madame Lateau, it seems, found no position so well suited to her needlework as just in the doorway of Louise's room, and from this place she never moved the whole afternoon, so that visitors were obliged to stumble over her in order to enter. As to Rosine and Adeline, their conduct is such that all Christians must hope that the prophecy of Palma, the ecstatica of Oria in Louise's regard will be speedily fulfilled. Palma declares that the day is not far distant when Louise will be removed from the society of those whose conduct necessarily fetters her spiritual advancement.

Rosine Lateau, as it is well known, took occasion to inform one of the exiled princesses of Italy—the same one, if we mistake not, who lately electrified the world by leaving all things to follow Our Lord, in the humble garb of a Franciscan nun—that, in the sight of God, she, the princess, was no more than one of themselves. A sentiment, which would have been lovely humility in the princess, but which, coming from the mouth of the seamstress, savored more of rebellious envy than becomes the true Christian. Only the plea of extreme ignorance could in this case excuse Rosine, for certainly those whose exile has the same origin, nay, is identical with the trials and imprisonment of the Holy Father, must be very dear to God, and it would seem presumption to claim any equality with them, either temporal or spiritual.

Adeline had not as yet distinguished herself by any one remarkable action, but our experience proved that she is worthy to be the daughter of her mother and the sister of Rosine, however unfitted she may be to be the companion of one destined to take a place in the highest choir of the heavenly host.

The astonishing rudeness of this highly-favored family must be ascribed to the fact that, as before remarked, they were in utter ignorance of the miracles of Stigmata and Ecstasy, until they saw them exemplified in their own family. It is difficult for them to realize, when they deemed themselves well instructed in all pertaining to the Church, when they were proud to think whatever differences there might be in social position, religion made us all equals, that there was anything old in the history of religion which, when withheld from the masses, it was still impossible to conceal from the upper circles of education. Now, in spite of all argument and all instruction, they will speak of their sister's condition as "this new illness," very much in the same manner as Catholics in the United States will, in conversation, speak of the present chain of miraculous events in Europe, as a new glory added to the Church—

whereas, it is merely that they are just beginning to realize the existence of that particular phase of Church history.

Louise's family having no conception of the spiritual honor, they are tempted to feel that she suffers from ulcers and fits, and that all the world comes to gaze with heartless curiosity. Then they are foolishly annoyed by the reports that reach them of the remarks made by the infidel journals; they learn that they are accused of practising a deception, in order to enrich themselves, and, not having sufficient humility to endure the charge in holy silence, they wreak their displeasure on those who, by coming to see Louise, are the indirect causes of the excitement in her regard.

In view of all this, it is very difficult to make them accept the alms necessary for three women, forced to gain their living without any masculine aid whatever. Once a lady who had been present during Louise's ecstasy, seeing the extreme poverty of the family, wished to give Madame Lateau a small sum to provide herself with some useful articles of which the cottage was destitute. Madame Lateau refused it angrily, roughly pushing away the lady's outstretched hand.

Finally, perhaps because the ruinous condition of her house afforded too many crevices of which the curious could avail themselves on Friday, Madame Lateau permitted Gregoire Lateau's former employers to repair the cottage, or rather to rebuild it, on account of—*the faithful services of her husband.*

Up to the day of her death, it was a continual interior struggle for Madame Lateau to realize the miraculous character of her daughter's sufferings. One week, asserting her belief that the doctors and the priests were employing medical secrets to torment her daughter, she exerted her authority as mistress of the house, and forbade the entrance of anyone on the following Friday, not even excepting Dr. Lefebvre, whom she had hitherto regarded with complete confidence; M. Niels might come in the morning to administer Holy Communion to Louise, as the Holy Viaticum always seemed to refresh her so greatly, but he was to leave immediately afterwards, and not to show himself there again the whole day. Neighbors and strangers were alike excluded, and the mother and her two daughters were left to face alone all the horrors of those dreadful torments.

Those who remember having nursed some member of their family through a painful illness, without receiving one visit of sympathy, can form a slight notion of the position in which these three had placed themselves. Louise herself had an opportunity of undergoing one portion of the Passion, namely: The solitude and desolation; for there was no one to have compassion upon her, no one to watch even one hour with her. Unassisted by the usual atmosphere of prayer which filled her cottage on other Fridays, Louise had to experience the most excessive suffering that the human frame can endure.

Just the morning of that Friday, which Dr. Lefebvre expected to spend in Louvain, he was called to the bedside of one of his regular patients, then passing sometime at a country seat not far from Bois d'Haine. Finding himself thus accidentally in the neighborhood of the house which he had been forbidden to approach, he ventured to present himself, quite late in the afternoon however, at Madame Lateau's door. With the penetration of the educated classes, he had surmised that by that time even Madame Lateau's iron nerves would be glad to be soothed by some communication with the outer world. He was welcomed by all with a heartiness which far exceeded any previous experience of his professional career. Far from having abated her daughter's sufferings, Madame Lateau's course of action had visibly augmented them, and she never cared to repeat her ingenious experiment. It did serve to make her slightly more amenable to reason; amiable resignation to her would have been an impossibility. Certainly her shortcomings in relation to the miraculous condition of her daughter must have resulted from an ignorance truly invincible;

probably God forgave them all, man had surely much to excuse.

At the same time that M. le Curé had granted the permission to see Louise, he had been very explicit with regard to the hour of the daily Mass in the church of Bois d'Haine, and it was evident that he hoped we would attend Mass there on Thursday morning. There had been a time when we were exceedingly anxious to witness every phase of the wonders of Bois d'Haine, but by the time that we left Tournay we were in a perfectly passive condition, and every subsequent effort might almost be styled mechanical. When our desire was the greatest, we believed just as earnestly as did Simon de Montfort or St. Louis in the power of God and the existence of modern miracles; but the nineteenth century is not the thirteenth, and in our native land public opinion does not even desire to claim that public faith which reigned in Christian Europe six hundred years ago, that universal belief which is necessary for the frequency of miracles, and we did so long to feel and realize by means of our senses that God still manifests His power to man. Had either St. Louis, or the brave Simon de Montfort, dwelt in an un-Catholic land, they would not have so immediately and so willingly relinquished the chances of witnessing a miracle; for a mere intellectual effort of belief, unsustained by any tangible surroundings, is most wearisome. Had they belonged to the nineteenth century, while still indifferent concerning the gratification of their curiosity, they would have accepted every opportunity of increasing their ability to testify to the truth of the operations of Divine Providence.

It was with the latter spirit that we were filled, while at Bois d'Haine. We were willing to make every exertion in our power, willing that our efforts should fail, satisfied that if it would be for the honor and glory of God, or for our own salvation, success was certain. Animated purely by these sentiments, we discussed the advisability of witnessing Louise receive Holy Communion in church on the day previous to her sufferings, or on Saturday morning, when we would be more certain to recognize her. Since then this feeling of utter indifference has changed into one of hearty rejoicing at having been permitted to witness as much as we did, for thus we became the means of consoling other believing hearts with the assurance of the reality of those wonderful tidings whose vaguest rumors causes a feeling of awe to fill the pious mind. How often have we been either directly or indirectly the means of turning the tide of incredulous and flippant conversation concerning that "young girl in Belgium!" Can we ever sufficiently thank Mgr. Dumont and M. Niels for having allowed us the privilege of giving our testimony!

As we had decided to wait until Saturday to attend Mass in Bois d'Haine, Thursday morning we went to the church in Fayt. There we heard a style of High Mass very frequently celebrated in Belgium; a well-trained adult chorister, having a place on the Epistle side, sings without the aid of any instrument the

Kyrie, Gloria and *Credo,* to slow, long drawn-out notes, which some would style Gregorian, although it differs greatly from Roman or Italian Gregorian. There is nothing in this music to scandalize the most decorous Puritan, and if we were to consider music merely as an aid to devotion, this would be infinitely preferable to mere imitations of fine compositions.

After breakfast, we returned to our books which, although unsuited to our national and individual peculiarities, possessed an interest amounting to fascination, owing to the close proximity of the scene of the events narrated. To read Louise's Life, not only in lands where the church walls, covered with numberless *ex votos*, tell of constant miracles, both small and great, but where the sound of the Angelus ringing in Bois d'Haine can reach the ear, where the green tree tops fail to hide its belfry from the eye, is altogether different from poring over its pages when the waves of the Atlantic are rolling between you and that land where you are told there exists a certain hamlet of Bois d'Haine, which you have failed to find on the most minute map of Europe within your reach.

Knowledge obtained through the sense of sight, even in its most direct operations, is often undervalued; therefore, it is not surprising that the advantages derived from viewing merely the scene of any action should be often ignored, but without leaving Belgium we find a striking example of the greatness of these advantages when applied to historical purposes. What amateur or proficient in military tactics, having means and opportunity, has failed to visit the field of Waterloo? Having visited it, who will pretend that he understood all the minutiæ of the contest, or even realized the existence of a Waterloo precisely as well by the mere use of maps and plans? By the time that, by these latter means, the mind has fully mastered all the topographical details, the brain is too wearied to draw any just conclusion, or, at least, it becomes very difficult to clear it sufficiently for it to be able to dwell on any subject requiring concentration of thought.

Akin to this depreciation of the advantages of the eye is the popular idea, that reading can fully supply the place of seeing, but in our own individual cases we always found that it was impossible for any description, however accurate, to produce the same distinct idea as that given by means of vision. Often, in the course of our travels, the explicit and familiar expressions of our guide-book brought to our mind's eye bright pictures of beautiful or sublime scenery, but no matter how carefully we, then well-practiced in that species of mental exercise, had entered into every detail of anticipated pleasure, the excursion presented prominent features of which our planning had not afforded us even a glimpse. The waters of the picturesque Alpine lake, washed shores, whose attractions had been but imperfectly grasped by the mind, for the words chestnut groves, vineyards, olive orchards, distant glaciers, etc., had merely suggested outlines, and utterly failed to prepare us for the added pleasures of the ear, such as a chorus of church bells from the half a hundred hamlets buried in the surrounding mountains, ringing the Angelus at day dawn. The sombre rocky defile, with its foaming, dashing torrent, looked far otherwise than our admiration had depicted it; and even if our faithful guide-book had told us that a cross was planted on the highest peak of that region, we were always unprepared for the full effect of sunlight and shadow on the barren summit piercing the clouds to bear aloft into the blue heavens, the token of man's gratitude for Redemption and Salvation.

The principle involved in these two paragraphs, and which is so perfectly applicable to history and natural scenery, serves admirably to illustrate one manner in which grace performs its noiseless work at shrines and at places hallowed by being the scene of holy actions. One may learn a great many lessons from the life of St. Francis by the reality imparted to it in seeing Assisi, often in the summer evenings watching from the heights of Perugia the sunset glow fade away from the green valley of the Tiber, had we learned something new about Cherubim and Seraphim, we knew not how, but it seemed to be just by gazing at the time-stained walls of Assisi, gilded by the parting light of day. If that which took place six centuries since can spread almost in the very atmosphere a holy unction, a grace of teaching, how much louder can grace whisper to the heart where holy things are actually taking place! Never had the brown walls of Assisi, basking in the warm sunshine of an Umbrian summer, made us realize as did the cottages of Bois d'Haine, that there have dwelt, and do dwell on earth chosen souls destined to take their places among the Seraphim, and to dwell forever in the very furnace of the fires of Divine Love.

There was a time in the lives of some of us, when the knowledge of our religion was more the result of our own efforts and a species of mental victory, then, although we knew that by Redemption, we were called to the company of the Angelic hosts, (Heb. xii, 22), yet we had a fixed idea that in Heaven man would be entirely separate from the nine choirs of the heavenly hierarchies, having very little in common with them, save in adoring God for all eternity. By degrees, as we came more and more under the influence of that silent teaching, which, in the very act of conquering the intellect, elevates it to a higher standard than any of which it had ever dared to dream, we learned to understand how man will take the places of the third, who were cast out of Heaven by the sword of Michael the Archangel, (Apoc. xii, 9). Assisi told us the real meaning of that blessed word predestination, explained how all of us, free to win eternal life, were yet each one called to win it differently, because predestined not only to different choirs, but to different places—places which it will be our everlasting glory to win, or our *own* everlasting shame to lose.

Thus, also, was a new light thrown on vocation, showing that our individual duties, however petty, and apparently of little moment to our fellow-men, are the hammer and anvil to shape us so that we will be able to take our appointed places among Angels or Archangels, Principalities or Powers—to be of their number, to be like them, yet differing from them just as new recruits when mingled with veterans are uniformed like them, and yet lack some distinguishing mark which designates him who has served even from the beginning. Then, we saw how very impossible it is for the veneration of saints to foster a spiritual ambition, a desire of the fame of sanctity similar to the ambition of an Alexander, a Cæsar, or a Bonaparte; for the very life that calls for pious admiration shows us clearly that, unless that wonderful life is foreordained for us, we may not presume to imitate more closely that which seems beyond human endurance.

All this Assisi taught us, but it remained for Bois d'Haine to make it a living reality; and Bois d'Haine had its own special lessons. Just as far as the distinctions of worldly importance separate the Belgian hamlet from Assisi—the home of nobles and princes—so far, in the eyes of man, is the peasant maiden from the son of the wealthy merchant; she, the servant of the class of which he was the favorite companion; she, who has nothing to lose of this world's goods—he, who had all that riches could give—yet they are both called by God to that choir over which the human nature of Our Lord presides, that choir which man cannot enter, save by enduring the sufferings of the Crucifixion. Do not these two examples teach us the manner in which God overlooks the social barriers intended to preserve order in the world's economy? Are we not shown that it is not by the almost entire exclusion of either high or low from the number of the chosen, but by impartial selections from all classes? St. Francis, the rich patrician; St. Catharine, of Sienna, the daughter of a poor fuller; St. Catharine, of Genoa, in whose veins flowed blood almost royal; and Louise Lateau, the child of poor peasants—do not they form a group which completely explains how God has no regard for the countenance of the rich, nor for the person of the indigent? (Lenticus xix, 15).

When we had exhausted our capability of meditating on these lessons, we indulged in a few speculations concerning those who would be admitted with us. Some doctors there would be, of course—perhaps even non-Catholic physicians; for those learned in medicine were by no means slow to avail themselves of the opportunities of inquiry which were so frankly and so generously given—it was only the medical faculty of Berlin that openly refused to recognize the freedom allowed to science by the ecclesiastical authorities.

Of its members, Virchow was the one who personified all its insolence; not many months before our visit to Bois d'Haine, he had astounded the public by the extraordinary terms which he proposed to Louise's superiors. Refusing to visit her cottage, he would examine into the matter only on condition that Louise would enter his hospital totally unattended by any member of her own family, by any relative, by any friend or acquaintance, or by anyone whom she, her family or her friends would select. Only a thorough infidel, and one who defied every moral and religious safeguard, could have dared to make these proposals. Who is there among those familiar with the lives of the saints who is not reminded of certain passages in the acts of the virgin martyrs, one of which is commemorated in the church of St. Agnes in Piazza Navona, in Rome? In the case of Louise the defending angels were represented by Madame Lateau and her two older daughters, who did not give either Louise or her superiors any chance to refuse these impertinent propositions. It is to be hoped that Virchow received their reply just as it fell from their lips.

We had concluded that, since it was so intensely disagreeable for Rosine and Adeline to see people passing their house, they might make remarks to M. Niels, which might be calculated to render him a little impatient with us, and that, therefore, it would be better for us to abstain from going again to Bois d'Haine before Friday; but we suddenly remembered that, although in granting the permission M. le Curé had named the hour, he had not told the place of rendez-vous. Since one would be obliged to pass by, all three might as well commit the offence; so we started on our double errand— a walk for health and pleasure, and a visit to the church. As we passed the Lateau cottage, we heard an animated conversation, and we saw a priest peering through the white curtains; thus, when we reached the parish house, we were not surprised to hear that M. Niels had gone to see Louise Lateau. After our devotions were finished, and we were returning to Fayt, we met M. le Curé, who accosted us with a reproof for passing so often by Louise's house.

"Her sisters tell me that you are continually passing and repassing; you mustn't do that, it annoys them."

"M. le Curé," was the reply, "we passed her house when we came to apply for admission, again when you sent us to the Hotel de la Poste, and then again twice by coming to visit the Blessed Sacrament yesterday afternoon—you know that in Fayt the church is closed in the afternoon."

In the estimation of M. Niels, or of any other European pastor, a daily visit to the Blessed Sacrament is so essential an act of an ordinary Christian life, that he would as soon have thought of telling us to omit our morning or evening prayers out of deference to any particular person's prejudice, as to say that, since it annoyed Louise's sisters, we would have done much better to have refrained from the performance of this devotion; therefore, his manner changed completely the moment he received the answer quoted.

M. le Curé was then informed of our version of the little adventure of the preceding evening, and how violently the woman slammed the door, as if she feared that we would force our entrance.

"That was one of Louise's sisters," said M. le Curé; "she told me that you would have entered had she not shut the door—but you did not wish to do so, did you?" To the question as to where we would meet him on the following day, he replied:

"At Louise's door, stand in front of the house until I bid you enter. It will be very crowded to-morrow, besides which, there will be many whom I shall be obliged to send away. I wonder how I shall manage it all! I had no intention of admitting you; I would not have done so if Monseigneur had not said that about really wishing it, but he did say, '*Je le desire vivement.*'"

With this characteristic speech on his lips, M. Niels lifted his broad-brimmed hat, and bade us good evening; and we returned to Fayt to find ourselves just in time for the supper at the table d'hôte.

In Belgium the word table d'hôte has not lost its original signification of the "landlord's own table." Although among other nations on the Continent it means the formal full meals served according to set rule in several courses, over which the landlord may or may not preside, but of which he never partakes, in Belgium the traveller sits down to the same bountiful repast that is spread before mine host, his wife and their older children. All those who are thus partaking of the table d'hôte are expected to join freely in general conversation. In the larger towns a party, especially when composed chiefly of ladies, may, without giving offence, secure an agreeable privacy by choosing another hour and a more simple repast, but in a small place like Fayt such an act would be regarded as a direct insult to the family of the landlord, and to the other lodgers.

On this particular evening we found the usual number of persons at the table, augmented by several invited guests, and, in addition, the élite of the neighborhood began to assemble in the dining-room. From their conversation we discovered that the young gentlemen of the vicinity are in the habit of coming every Thursday evening to the Hotel de la Poste to inspect those who are going to visit Louise, and then they all make it a point to loiter around the railway station at Menage every Friday afternoon, in order to listen to the conversation of those who leave immediately after witnessing her ecstasy. Naturally, after an hour thus spent in watching the course of that astonishing miracle, the nervous system will be too overwrought for the lips to be very guarded in their utterance. Thus, by listening repeatedly on these occasions, the young men of Fayt hope ultimately to solve the problem which is agitating the minds of those living near Bois d'Haine.

This puzzling problem is not any of the supernatural phases of the subject; for all of these the young men of Fayt and Menage quietly accept as positive facts, which they have not the slightest inclination to doubt, and which, although the casual observer of their conduct might not readily infer, are a source of grace to them. Neither did they concern themselves with any of the metaphysical questions arising from one style of considering the matter, though they were probably as capable of discussing abstruse subjects as many who flood the popular journals with enigmatical writing. Their problem is purely natural, and its terms are comprehensible to the most ordinary mind, namely: How may a person gain admittance to the cottage of Louise Lateau? As yet it remained unsolved, but the young men, and some, too, who had arrived at an age supposed to be more discreet, were very busy fastening the links in the chain of evidence by which they hoped to arrive at a definite conclusion; but many open questions remained. Was the sacerdotal character the "open sesame?" By no means; every week priests were refused, and laymen accepted, though belonging to the laity was not infallible admission, nor were priests always excluded. Was it riches? Was it poverty? Often the rich were sent away, and the poor admitted; or the rich had freedom to enter, and the poor were told to wait. Recommendations were often required, but even when these came from the highest quarters, M. Niels could disregard them, and grant the request of those having no introduction whatever. The length of the journey taken by the person to reach Bois d'Haine seemed to make no impression on its pastor, neither was the plea of a long residence in the neighborhood of any avail.

The discussion of this problem drew forth many anecdotes, which demonstrated that M. Niels did not possess that delicate, sensitive frame of mind and temperament that would render it keen torture to come in constant contact with the rough natures by which he was surrounded, of which poor Mme. Lateau and her two older daughters were prominent examples. At the conclusion of tales, which show that M. Niels knew how to unite a certain degree of physical force to moral suasion, in defending Louise from unwelcome intrusion, the strangers would gaze around the company, hoping to read in the faces of some a denial—at least, in part—but, although the older ones might look reprovingly at the thoughtless youth, who had been lacking in that perfect reverence (considered so important by all American Catholics), still they would answer the look of inquiry with the words *C'est vrai.*

In the midst of this discussion the landlady, who had been absent a few moments, re-entered the room, saying in a low tone :

"Here is a doctor who will be permitted to see Louise all day to-morrow."

As she finished these words, a young man, apparently just beginning the third decade of his life, entered the room. Gracefully acknowledging the presence of those already seated at the table, and taking the place allotted him by the landlady, a few introductory words from her placed him on speaking terms with all the assembled company. It took but a glance for us to see, from the scrupulous attention to dress, the carefully brushed hair, parted—as we would say—like a lady's, that here was one who did not take what the Puritan band of Plymouth Rock would have called "a truly serious view of life." All traces of Puritanical notions on matters of apparel had been rather well-effaced from our minds, and there was no special prejudice to prevent us from reading in his face the indelible marks of the Sacraments, and the countless other effects of the steady practices of a Christian life without affectation. By this time we had thoroughly learned that, of course, with the exception of very peculiar vocations, true religion does not destroy all the sources of joy in the human heart, neither does she ruthlessly uproot what the world calls foibles; for these are generally qualities, which only need a little training, a little pruning, in order to grow into means of grace and salvation. Why, for example, eradicate the love of adventure, which, when well directed, will sustain the explorer in his laudable task of seeking to enrich the stores of man's acquired knowledge, or—to ascend still higher—that which may be one of the sparks to kindle the zeal of the missionary? At the same time that we received these lessons, we were also made to understand that there is more humility in an apparent frivolity than in endeavoring to appear old beyond one's years; and thus we were not as scandalized as some might have been, at the light manner in which the gentlemen of Fayt had spoken of Bois d'Haine—for we saw that in the depths of their hearts was hidden the germ which could bring forth fair fruit in due season, and we were sure that grace would do her work with greater facility, because there was no hollow pretence of perfection.

Perhaps the young doctor was a fairer type than these of the Catholic youth of Europe, who, not always precisely frivolous, have not enough of absurd pride to wish to seem above harmless imperfection, and who have so little of that which is truly harmful on their consciences. Had he not been thoroughly pious, he would have been tempted to consider his chances of witnessing the miraculous condition of Louise Lateau in the light of the great adventure of his life; as it was, he was overcome by excitement, which found an escape-valve in voluble conversation. In a very short time we all knew that, by a special recommendation from Dr. Lefebvre, he had obtained the fullest privileges ever granted to medical inquiry, and that already, in the company of M. Niels, he had visited Louise in her cottage.

"But isn't she ugly, though!" was the exclamation that terminated the torrent of speech with which he had inundated us. This remark was received by complete silence, and the doctor's face expressed great astonishment when he found that this sentiment was not echoed by anyone.

"You are all, no doubt, familiar with her ordinary appearance," said he, after a little pause: "but I was disappointed, I expected to find something—some pleasant expression to redeem plain features; but I saw in her nothing but a Flemish peasant maid. M. Niels and I entered the cottage, and I saw two peasant girls—just nothing but peasants, sitting together and chatting in a very lively manner; and M. Niels said:

"'Now, which of these two girls do you take to be Louise?'

"'Neither one nor the other, M. le Curé,' said I, very confidently.

"'Nevertheless,' said he, 'one of them is Louise.'

"I was puzzled, I assure you. Finally, I recollected that Louise always wears half mittens to conceal the slight marks of the stigmata, and that was my only clue. You who live in the neighborhood must see her very often?"

"Oh, we are never admitted! No one present has ever seen her since her present condition," replied one gentleman.

"You are awaiting your turn to witness the miracle, I understand that, but you must sometimes meet her in the street, or on the road?"

"Oh, never!" was the universal exclamation. "Not now; in former times we may have often seen her—but who thought anything about Louise Lateau, the sewing girl? Now she seems to be animated by an intense desire to hide herself from all strangers, and that means everyone not a resident of Bois d'Haine. We of Fayt are as much strangers to her as people from America; when we meet her by accident in Bois d'Haine, she runs into the nearest house, and everyone in the hamlet willingly helps her to conceal herself, so we never catch more than a glimpse of her."

Then followed various explanations of this strange conduct, which may be condensed thus. There have been occasions on which Louise has been accosted on the highway by persons unknown to her, among whom, the reader will regret to hear, have been those of her own sex, who have loaded her with abuse, giving a most vile explanation of her sufferings, and accusing her of wishing, by a shameful fraud, to stir up the people. Thus do the unbelieving help to heighten the resemblance between her and her Divine Master. Added to this, her sisters are always watching strangers, and putting unamiable interpretations on their actions, and Louise necessarily must be influenced by their ill-natured conversation, although it may not meet with her approval. Is it so very surprising after all, that the recollection of insults should cause her to fear and shun everyone of whose friendship she is not positively certain?

"I have never seen Louise yet, although M. le Curé has assured me that my turn will soon arrive," said a gentlemen whom we had met at every meal at the Hotel de la Poste—one of the "iron men" of the neighborhood. "You know," said he, appealing to the landlord, "how very often my business obliges me to pass through Bois d'Haine two and three times daily. Now very often I pass through the village so intent on my duties that I do not think of Louise; you know, considering the nature of those duties, that could well be. Sometimes before I have even thought, 'I am in Bois d'Haine,' I see a black figure hastily disappearing in a house; then I know I have seen Louise, whom I would not otherwise have remarked."

"Well, well," said the doctor, "her condition has given her a notoriety so far from agreeable in many particulars, that I for my part do not wonder that she wishes to conceal herself from curious eyes, and that she shrinks from everyone save her old friends."

"As far as I have read," said our mother,

"it is you doctors who torment her with all your investigations. There is but one experiment that you have failed to make; you have not sent her on an ocean voyage to discover if, since she does not eat, it would be possible for her to be seasick. Had she a perfect horror of all doctors I could readily comprehend the reason."

The young man blushed, as he replied in a low voice, "Madame, what you say is but too true."

"As to this matter of her not eating," said the landlord, who having been, like his wife, denied access to Louise's cottage, took every opportunity to express a peevish incredulity, "I don't believe it at all. Why," added he, helping himself to an enormous slice of cold roast, "it is perfectly impossible!"

The doctor, whose own appetite had been sharpened by the journey from Louvain, as well as by excitement, and under whose knife and fork the viands were disappearing as rapidly as was consistent with gentlemanly manners, regarded mine host for an instant with a look of keen amusement, before replying laughingly, " Certainly for you, and for me."

"That is what I find so incredible," said the gentleman before quoted. "I can understand the stigmata; that is a miracle, it is true, but still comprehensible. But how is it possible for anyone to exist without eating?"

"Let me tell you," said the doctor gently, "that of all the conditions under which Louise exists, the only one that is totally inexplicable by all the laws of science is this miracle of the stigmata, for there are decided marks separating it entirely from the cases to which those unlearned in medicine might think it parallel. Whereas, save that, nowhere in the annals of medicine has the duration of sleeplessness, existence without food, etc., been so extended as in the present example, there are cases on record where, in individuals, life has been sustained for long intervals without these generally indispensable aids. So if you believe in the stigmata, all else should be easily credited."

If American Catholics would reflect for a few moments, they would not find this particular effect of the Holy Eucharist so totally unexampled in their own experience, although they may never have seen any development of it that they could positively term miraculous. That the reception of Holy Communion can sustain the body in the endurance of extraordinary bodily fatigue, as well as support the soul under affliction, but few will deny; that it sometimes partially takes the place of ordinary nourishment is not readily acknowledged, yet the majority of us need not leave our own social circle to find one or two examples of this miraculous effect of the Holy Eucharist operating in a lesser degree. Though God does not always choose that this power shall be exhibited, and we have no right to make its appearance a test of sanctity, much less its non-appearance a proof of an unworthy reception.

When the doctor had perceived that the people of the neighborhood were so utterly excluded from the wonders operated in their midst, he had, from motives of politeness, refrained from continuing the account of his call at Louise's cottage, but when asked for other particulars he gave them freely, mixing them with exclamations at her lack of beauty. We could not help being greatly amused at the naive manner with which he expressed his surprise at this, and we thought that for him it was very well the Almighty had not, when He so adorned Louise's soul, added earthly beauty, for the doctor's religious sentiments would have had still greater difficulty in overcoming his strong inclination to regard his present opportunities as a startling adventure.

When he was introduced to her by M. Niels, Louise treated him with a great deal of confidence, and answered all his questions with the utmost frankness. To the question, did she really live without nourishment? she replied:

"It is a long time since I have felt the need of food, and now I am permitted, since I do not feel any desire for food, to abstain from taking it."

"Are you disgusted with it when you see it?" was the next question.

"Not at all," she said, "I think very little of it; all I know is that I do not wish for it."

"Do you never desire it?" asked the doctor. "Now I hear you often cook for the others; don't you wish for it when you are preparing it?"

"Never," answered she, "no more than if I had just eaten a hearty meal."

"And are you well and strong in spite of this extraordinary fact?" asked he.

To her response in the affirmative, he enquired if it was true that she could carry her sewing machine, without assistance, to any part of the house.

"Oh, yes," she replied, and suiting the action to the word, she lifted the heavy tailor's machine and carried it with ease to another part of the room, a task which the doctor would have found difficult. He then asked to see her hands, and she removed her mittens, showing hands roughened by work and very slightly scarred by what appeared to have been a wound, extending from the palm to the upper surface.

"And as I saw her well and strong," he added, "so she is every day of the week with the exception of Friday. To-morrow I accompany M. le Curé when he goes to administer Holy Communion to her as Viaticum. I must own that I am anxious to see the change."

From this the reader will understand that during many years of the wonderful part of her life Louise was not subject to constant stigmatisation. She did not immediately take her place among that class of helpless suffering to which the Tyrolese ecstatica Maria Mörl belonged, so that, unlike St. Lidwina, she was not dependent on the caprices of those around her. This was not clearly understood in America; from the very beginning Louise was spoken of as a constant invalid, and about the time of our own visit to Bois d'Haine a report was in circulation on this side of the Atlantic that Louise had been prevented from receiving Holy Communion by her family; in consequence, the stigmatisation had ceased, and she was able to rise from bed, and that each time she made use of her regained strength to elude the vigilance of her friends in order to receive Holy Communion, and it would immediately restore her to her suffering condition, which was repeatedly cured by the systematic refusal of her sisters to allow the Blessed Sacrament to enter the house. If Catholics had reflected but a moment they would have recognized the falseness of this report, and by reading the authentic notices of her life they will see that the Holy Communion is her chief source of relief and consolation. That she should receive Holy Communion daily cannot be necessary for the continuance of the miracle, for as the reader will remember Louise was only a weekly communicant when the stigmata first made their appearance. If the miracle is now dependent on the daily reception of the Holy Eucharist, and if God wills that the miracle should continue, in the spiritual condition, or rather degree, at which Louise has arrived, she could receive Holy Communion without human intervention, as the friends of God have frequently done; for example, St. Stanislaus Kostka, and at the present day Palma d'Oria.*

Every report concerning Louise Lateau should be carefully compared with the authentic accounts of her life and her condition, and if there is any startling discrepancy between the report and these accounts, American Catholics will do well not to pay attention to remarks which may perhaps be drawn originally from non-Catholic European journals, or from other sources opposed to the cause of religion. It is true in all the years that have elapsed since Louise Lateau has been leading this remarkable life that there have been some Fridays, few in number, on which no stigmatisation took place, but these exceptions were apparently without cause, for

---

*The perusal of Section VI, Book 4, of Faber's work on the Blessed Sacrament will throw a great deal of light on prolonged abstinence and miraculous Communions. From this admirable chapter one may see that to deprive Louise Lateau of the Blessed Eucharist would make her ill instead of restoring her to health, as it would be a course of starvation for her.

they occurred when nothing had been done to separate Louise from external influences.

This Thursday evening our landlady had just commenced to superintend the removal of the dishes, when there came another representative of the upper circles of Fayt and Menage— a gentleman whose careful toilet showed how affectionately he clung to the youth of which his apparel was the only relic. After responding to the welcome given him by his acquaintances, he bestowed a hasty glance at the doctor and at ourselves.

"Well," said he, as he seated himself; "last Friday there were here to see Louise Lateau thirty persons, of whom fifteen went as they came. Among these last was an English gentleman and his lady, who had brought a letter from their own Archbishop, whose personal friends they are, to our Archbishop, who gave them a recommendation to M. Niels. Thus doubly fortified, they presented themselves at Bois d'Haine, and — M. le Curé refused them unconditionally! It seems that the lady endeavored to expostulate, and M. le Curé showed them the door, saying, 'I told you *no*, go away.' I saw them at the railway—the lady is extremely well bred, excessively well bred. And that they should have been thus treated!"

"What! refuse Mgr. Dechamps!" exclaimed one of his hearers.

"Oh, that is nothing!" said another; "he has done that many a time, and he is ready to do that at any time—but to tell a lady, '*allez-vous-en!*'"

"And such a lady," said the gentleman who related the incident, and on whom the good-breeding of the Englishwoman had made a profound impression; "I am very sure it is the first time that she was ever told to take herself out of a house."

"So he refused Mgr. Dechamps!" said a third. "I hear that these ladies are admitted at the request of Mgr. de Tournay—has M. Niels ever refused Mgr. Dumont?"

"Ah! but Mgr. Dumont's come but rarely! Perhaps M. Niels knows that," said one of the first speakers.

"I tell you," said the landlord, "whose recommendation he won't refuse, and that is—money. Let your Englishman give him a hundred francs, and then he may see Louise."

"You know better than that," said the full chorus of voices; "what does M. Niels care for donations? They come without his troubling himself to change his course of action."

"Yes," said one; "you know that M. —— did offer M. Niels a hundred francs, and M. Niels threw it back at him. I would not like to be the man to couple my request to enter with a sum of money."

"We can all see," said another, "that fully one-half of those who gain admittance are not persons capable of making large donations, and we do know that the wealthy men of the iron works here, to whom a couple of hundred francs would be as nothing compared with their desire to see Louise, are forced to wait indefinitely for their turn to arrive."

Leaving, as we then did, this self-constituted council to solve the problem to which they probably have not as yet found the slightest clue, a few results of our own observation will be added as a conclusion of the subject.

Doubtless, M. Niels, like Gideon, has some simple covenant with himself by which he decides whom to accept and whom to reject. It is not improbable that the multitude who were ordered to return to their homes (Judges vii, 8), were as much bewildered by the seemingly arbitrary selection made by their leader as those whom M. Niels tells to go away are when they see those whom he chooses. The terms of this covenant may be few or many, but from all that we heard we are tolerably certain that, unless he has it already, no one who pays a guide to conduct him to the parish house of Bois d'Haine will receive the desired permit. In our own case, M. Niels was very particular in his inquiries of how the way had been found. As far as donations are concerned, M. Niels receives so many that he is callous to their influence—not but that if anyone made him a handsome present for the Church, M. Niels would not sooner or later give a permit, but the gift must not assume the nature of a bribe; therefore, let those who are accustomed to work their way to prominence and influential position on account of large donations, be very, very cautious how they approach M. Niels. If your means have barely sufficed to bring you to Bois d'Haine, but the vicinity of so great a miracle fills your heart with a pious desire to contribute to the monument that will perpetuate its memory, do not be ashamed to offer the little that you can spare to M. le Curé—for his is a disposition that will regard far more the *good will of the giver* than the *size of the gift*. He will not estimate the length of your purse by the length of your journey; there is no class of men more ready to allow you to judge of your own pecuniary resources than the clergy of Europe, and M. Niels would not know how to make himself an exception. Such as He on whom the lesson of the widow's mite is not lost, often despise the ostentatious gifts of wealth, while they welcome the simple offering of the poor—which brings most surely a blessing, perhaps a miracle of multiplication.

VIII.

NOT the faintest tinge of dawn had appeared in the east, when we were aroused by our landlady's voice as, tapping on the doctor's door, she added the words :

"Doctor, it is five o'clock."

"Yes, Madame."

A few moments later, quick, springing footsteps descended the stairway, soon to be succeeded by the sound of the street door closing softly, leaving the house to darkness and silence. This was all. But it chased sleep from our eyelids, and, mentally, we followed the doctor as hastening along the highway, he scarcely heeded the darkness or the raw, misty air. Thus, we saw him accompanying M. Niels into the church still filled with the gloomy shadows of night, faintly their tapers glimmered for an instant around the tabernacle, and then, vested in surplice and stole, the priest issued from the Gothic portal, followed by the doctor, who bore in one hand a votive light, in the other a warning bell—for, thank Heaven, this was a Christian land, and when God leaves His home in the tabernacle to visit the dying and the bed-ridden, the sick and the suffering, He is not obliged to hide Himself from contempt and insult.

Where these were going we might not enter, but the variously worded descriptions of those who have been thus privileged unite to form but one distinct picture, and so we knew what greeted the eyes of priest and doctor as they entered Louise's chamber. Gradually since midnight the wounds, one by one, had opened, and now all the marks of the physical sufferings of the Passion were visible. Have you ever seen the four celebrated *Ecce Homo* of the Corsini gallery in Rome—the works of four among the greatest artists that Italy has produced? They are no marble fictions, but color has lent its powerful aid to make man realize the awful consequences of sin, and nothing is omitted; there are the bloody thorns, the shabby purple mantle, the livid wounds caused by the brutal stripes, and each of these paintings is the more perfect in proportion as it approaches more nearly the ideals of the Tyrolese artists, whose realistic representations so shock the sensitive minds of the majority of tourists. Have you ever seen Albrecht Dürer's, "Christ the Implorer of Souls?"* How the blood streams from that thorn-crowned head! And those frightful gashes in the clasped hands stretched forth in mute entreaty! Ah! that we had a few more of such productions of art! Perhaps, then, there would be a few more to exclaim, as we have heard those whose souls were touched by the grace dwelling in works such as these: "That was the way it really was!"

All such representations united, so those who have seen Louise at this hour tell us, barely

---

* Preserved in the gallery of the Moritz Kapelle, Nuremberg, sometimes called Dürer's *Ecce Homo*.

succeed in producing the same profound impression as that made by witnessing Louise's condition when she received the Holy Viaticum. Motionless, she kneels erect, insensible of all save pain; the blood flows from every wound, and drips from the marks of the invisible crown upon the linen cloth spread over her hands, on the fingers of the priest, perhaps on the Host Itself. Watch her as long as you may, each moment will bring the evidence of some previously unnoticed torture, and—that was the way it really was?

Oh, no! It is not barbarous; these representations are not the result of a savage taste, neither are they calculated to foster it. The share that man had in the original scene was barbarous, the torments were inflicted by men rendered savage through malice; sin, the cause of these torments, is still more savage, still more barbarous; and most barbarous of all is the manner in which we ungratefully shrink from anything that will remind us of what a God, made man for us, suffered for our redemption. We do not like to see the dreadful effects of our own sinful love of ease and pleasure pictured so forcibly to our eye; we wish to figure the Passion of Christ to ourselves in some dim, shadowy, poetic style that will not agitate our feelings so severely.

With us, as we waited that morning for daylight to appear, the vicinity of Louise Lateau gave our meditations a most realistic tendency, and a species of involuntary nature. Suggestions seemed to come rather from without than from within, and as we thought of Calvary itself, not an incident that could add to the suffering or to the ignominy seemed to escape us— the flaunting banners, the gay military trappings were all there; the expressions of the triumph of a foreign power over the Son of David, which was as deep an abyss of ignominy as the gibes of those who passed by; and when He was laid to rest by gentle, loving hands, there were gaping wounds that would not close, but seemed like mouths that will not be mute, crying aloud to the end of time, "Oh, my people!"

To frame to ourselves other ideals more consonant with our own notions of the dignity and majesty of the Divinity, would be imitating the Jews in their rejection of Our Lord because He did not accord with their preconceived ideas. We cannot regard the Passion of Our Lord in a poetical light; there is no poetry in it save in its own inherent sublimity—that sublimity which never, even in Isaias, reaches a height so lofty as when he describes the Man of Sorrows as utterly without comeliness and beauty, possessing nothing that could make us desirous of Him. " Despised, and the most abject of men." (Isaias liii, 3). So He appeared on Calvary, and so we must accept Him; for we have no right to make false gods to ourselves by imagining the mystery of the Redemption to have been accomplished in the slightest degree differently from " the way in which it really was." Had there been a better, a more sublime, a nobler method, it would have been chosen by the Eternal Wisdom.

With sentiments other than these it might be

dangerous to approach Bois d'Haine; for in no place could false sensitiveness receive so severe a shock as by contemplating this very realistic portrayal of the Mysteries of Calvary, and unless we are accustomed to think rightly concerning the passion of Christ, it would be well nigh impossible for us to learn the reasons why God chooses to have some of its phases so frequently repeated.

When the tardy daylight at length appeared, we were glad to rise and hasten to Mass, in which we would find refuge from the whirlwind of thought which was carrying us hither and thither. The morning hours rolled by slowly; for we could not read, neither did we care for conversation—as we were experiencing that dreadful feeling of unrest which is the result of expectation. Towards noon our landlady appeared at our door in a state of angry excitement, though we could discern that we were not the objects of her ire. She addressed us very pleasantly, bidding us come to our dinner.

"It won't be very palatable," said she; "for I failed to find any fish in the market. I have done my best with vegetables, eggs and sardines."

"I'll show them that that can't be done here," she muttered between her teeth. "'Privacy, indeed—in a great hurry!' So are these the same reasons for haste in both cases."

We followed her to the dining-room, scarcely understanding these last remarks; but as she opened the door for us we saw a group, whose appearance partially explained the displeasure of our hostess. Evidently this party—a blonde gentleman accompanied by two ladies—had wished to secure privacy by means of an early dinner, not knowing that this would constitute a first-class insult to the innkeepers and to their guests. A more quiet and unobtrusive pair than this fair-haired gentleman and the tall lady in mourning, whom we supposed might be his wife, are scarcely ever seen, but the lady who was with them was greatly elated at being in their society, and she lavished polite attentions on them, treating the gentleman with a deference only bestowed on those of royal descent.

Needless to say we did not altogether fancy the position in which our landlady had placed us, though we had no alternative but to take the places which she assigned us, opposite the offending group, at whom she darted an angry glance. The gentleman wore a large seal ring, which he concealed as soon as he perceived that it had attracted our attention, but not before we had detected the *fleur de lys*, among other specimens of heraldic zoology and botany. Hearing us speak to one another, he told the lady, who seemed to be the companion of the one whom we supposed to be his wife, to address us in our native language, perhaps to give us a polite warning that we would be understood. She spoke very fluently, with rather a harsh accent, but like one who feels at home in the use of foreign idioms. The lady in mourning, so she told us, had once before witnessed the miracle of Bois d'Haine; Dr. Lefebvre had been present, he had tested the wounds in Louise's hands, and he had proved that the wounds really penetrated the palm. This lady companion questioned us very closely concerning the doctor, expressing great disappointment because Dr. Lefebvre would not be present.

All this time that she was conversing with us, she did not pause in the least in her attentions to the gentleman whom she served to whatever was lacking on his plate before he had time to express any desire for it, and her deferential conduct differed greatly from the manner of the American hostess, begging her guests to take another cup of tea, etc., etc.

It annoyed the gentleman in no slight degree, for his present aim was to ignore his rank as much as possible, and as on the Continent American travelers have the reputation of making their republican notions but too apparent, even at the risk of offending the rules of politeness whenever the slightest occasion affords them the chance of proclaiming these principles, his annoyance was by no means lessened by our presence. We, on our part, wished as heartily as they could have done, that the landlady had respected their demands for privacy; for we had no desire to intrude ourselves upon persons whose rules of etiquette differed so widely from those which govern a republican society. We learned in this short half-hour to appreciate, in some degree, the feelings of the " help" at a gentleman's country residence, who, in sitting at the table with those whom she serves, finds herself unexpectedly surrounded by the manners and appliances of a life at complete variance with that by which she has always been surrounded. In the lady companion we probably saw the descendant of one who had been a faithful friend of some ancestor of the house of which the gentleman was a member. Admiration of a ruler, and personal friendship for him, when bequeathed as a legacy to posterity, unite to form the quality of unswerving loyalty in his descendants, and even the most intense republican that ever stood on American soil could not deny that it would be unjust and cruel to deprive this lady of a quality which afforded her such genuine happiness.

In one of her endeavors to show her devotion she overturned the castor, and its mingled contents streamed into their box of sardines, making a most loathsome compound. (As sardines were our principle article of food, that accident destroyed their dinner). The poor lady was utterly dismayed, and to console her the gentleman helped himself to a sardine, saying very pleasantly :

" Friday, at Bois d'Haine, one should be willing to do penance."

" Penance need not go to that extreme," remarked our mother; "there are sardines enough for all in our portion."

In obedience to this suggestion, one of us passed our supply to the lady, that she might repair the results of her awkwardness; in her excitement, she forgot to utter one word of thanks to us, but the gentleman, who never for a moment seemed to lose sight of the idea that he had no especial claims to deference from inhabitants of a republic, reminded her instantly of her neglect.

"You must thank the young lady; how does one say *merci* in English?"

"Thank you"—"*n'est-ce pas?*" said the lady in mourning, and he repeated the words after her.

They then conversed among themselves in French, the subjects being abstinence on Friday, and the Lenten fast; and we could perceive that the lady in mourning adhered to the most strict manner of observing them—that thoroughly fish and vegetable rule which never comes north of the Alps and the Pyrenees, and which, in fact, is only compatible with a mild climate and an early supply of native vegetables.

As this party arose to leave, the door behind us opened, and we heard slow footsteps approaching the table.

"Good day, ladies," said the doctor's voice.

As we turned to respond to the greeting, we

saw a very different being from the young exquisite of the evening before, and as he seated himself at the table there was not the slightest trace of the excitement with which he had begun his investigations. He was followed by an elderly gentleman (also a doctor), who was accompanied by his son—a youth of about twenty; the father had been already admitted upon the same footing as the other doctor; the son, like ourselves, awaited the hour of ecstasy. This doctor seemed inclined to converse upon the events of the morning, but our acquaintance replied with an evident reluctance—very different from his previous manner.

"One regrets to leave for a single moment," remarked the old gentleman at one stage of the conversation.

"I should not have left," replied he, "had not M. le Curé insisted that I should come to my dinner."

We looked at him as he ate slowly, and with that peculiarly deliberate manner which betokens how very far away thought is from that which is entering the mouth; and it seemed to us a miracle greater than Louise's total abstinence, that the body should be so thoroughly dependent on food as to oblige not only us, who were expecting to witness the miracle of which we had so vivid an idea, but also those who had been observing more than we expected to see, to take that nourishment whose operations, after all the explanations that men of science can give, are so mysterious and incomprehensible.

Although the reluctance of the young doctor to enter into any conversation whatever, much less to touch upon any of the events of the morning, was very evident, the old physician could not forbear uttering his thoughts aloud.

"Well; it is true," said he, "all that we are told is just so, and there is nothing like it in all the annals of medicine—it is not we who have to deal with such matters, is it?"

Instead of replying to him, the young doctor turned to us, and, speaking with an earnestness and a depth of reverential feeling which some persons would have been surprised to see a young man of his character exhibit, he exclaimed:

"Oh! madame, it is just as we read, only more wonderful—more wonderful! For it is impossible for any pen to describe all so accurately as to produce an impression sufficiently exalted."

Indeed, this was not difficult to believe; for he had come to Bois d'Haine thoroughly understanding all the details of the case, as far as it was in the power of written descriptions to impart knowledge, and yet this knowledge had failed to produce any visible change in him, at all comparable to that effected by actually seeing the miracle.

The next remarkable addition to our party was two theological students, who might have attained at the utmost the age of twenty; the decidedly triangular shape of their broad-brimmed hats, the graceful manner in which they wore the cloak and cassock, and the complete harmony of all the parts of their ecclesiastical costume, bespoke their peculiar right to be called Roman, and we were not surprised to hear that they were pursuing their studies at the Belgian College in Rome. They were now enjoying a vacation and a visit to their native land, and they had brought with them an introductory letter to M. Niels from the Prefect of the Propaganda—a recommendation which had procured them admittance to the hour of ecstasy.

The conversation now wandered away from the all-absorbing topic of interest, and assumed a character which Europeans love to style cosmopolite. This character is a natural consequence of the meeting of persons of different nations, and, therefore, is of frequent occurrence at hotel-tables and on the decks of steamers, whether these last be mere excursion boats or regular ocean packets, and he who is unable to understand all the variations of French by means of which cosmopolite ideas are expressed, misses many an agreeable opportunity of acquiring useful information. On this occasion the Roman students acquitted themselves very handsomely, and, without any unbecoming boldness, showed themselves thoroughly conversant with all the questions of the day, and even capable of giving information concerning matters of interest. One half-hour in their society would be a most powerful argument against all the slurs cast upon the system of education employed by Rome. By what means they had attained their intellectual development we are not prepared to state, but nowhere under the influence of that which the voice of liberal reform calls enlightened institutions do young men of nineteen and twenty show the same decided marks of mental culture.

"By the way," said the older doctor, "during a pause in the conversation, when you passed by Louise's house, was that English Archbishop still standing with his friends on the outside?"

The students, who were the ones addressed, replied in the affirmative, and asked one or two questions concerning this party.

"Why, ladies, true enough, I have something to tell you," said the young doctor. "You know that English gentleman and his lady concerning whom there was some conversation last evening? Who do you think it was that gave them that letter to Mgr. Dechamps? It was the Archbishop of Canterbury*—Dr. Manning himself! They have returned to-day, and Mgr. Manning is with them; he has made it a personal request to M. Niels, that this gentleman and his wife should be permitted to witness everything, but M. le Curé would not consent."

"Well!" interrupted one of the gentlemen of Fayt, "M. Niels has shown before this that it is very little he cares for Bishops or Archbishops, especially since he has been vested with indisputable authority in this matter."

"But," said the doctor, "it is not every

---

*At the time when the conversation above recorded took place, Dr. Manning then, not yet elevated to the Cardinalate, was among Europeans often called Archbishop of Canterbury—so often that it was easy to forget that, although Catholic primate of England, he was the incumbent of the new see of Westminster. Probably European Catholics versed in ecclesiastical history can never cease to regard the one who has inherited the powers of St. Dunstan, St. Anselm, and St. Thomas a Becket, as Archbishop of Canterbury. In order to make the Doctor's eulogy as comprehensible as it was applicable, his exact words are preserved.

Archbishop who is the Archbishop of Canterbury, and not every Archbishop of Canterbury has been a Dr. Manning! However, M. le Curé treats him with the utmost respect, offering *him* every opportunity of investigation, but he will not admit his friends on those same conditions."

"You know, don't you?" said the older doctor, "that M. Niels finally consented to allow the gentleman and his wife to be present during the hour of ecstasy—each a half-hour, in turn—and that was a great concession; for the number of those permitted to enter is unusually large to-day."

"They refused that," replied the other, "and Mgr. Manning will not enter at all unless he can secure to his friends precisely the same privileges which he enjoys. Now, these three are in the meadow opposite Louise's house, and they intend to watch all afternoon, and see what class of people are admitted—how it is all conducted, etc. It is certainly very noble for Archbishop Manning to stand by his friends so firmly."

"But how polite and kind M. le Curé is to us!" said the older gentleman, "and is it not wonderful to observe the instant change when he addresses some one with whom he chooses to be displeased?"

"Each time," replied his young colleague, "I congratulate myself on our singular luck, and I make a resolution to be still more circumspect in my conduct towards him; I should not enjoy that style of treatment."

There is nothing like the vicinity of holy places to promote a rapid acquaintance, to throw down what may be called the uncharitable restraints of society, and to cause people to realize the bonds of union created by a common participation of the Sacraments of the Catholic Church; therefore, when we all arose from the table the casual observer would have been surprised to learn that the acquaintance had been of so recent an origin. As the doctors left the room, they said very pleasantly to those admitted to the hour of ecstasy:

"*Au revoir, chez Louise.*"

There had been no further conversation concerning Cardinal Manning and his friends, but among ourselves we discussed the affair more freely. Perhaps, of all those then assembled at Bois d'Haine, we best understood the situation, which was occasioned by the meeting of two systems differing entirely one from the other. We remembered the close relations existing between clergy and laity in our own land—relations resulting in part from the extreme dependence of a Church disunited from the State, on the laity in general, and we now knew where this dependence did not exist that certain bonds of union between pastor and people were not only severed, but were also not in the least understood. M. Niels probably is one of those who cannot comprehend any of the good resulting from our system; thus, he could not believe that it was of any importance that lay persons should have the same opportunity of giving testimony to religious facts as the clergy. Were he told that there is a class of English-speaking Catholics to whom the voice of a layman would, in some things, carry more conviction than the word of an ecclesiastic, the good man would be horror-stricken, and certainly would do all in his power to thwart plans of concession to such persons.

There is certainly much that is beautiful in the relations which have subsisted between priest and people in lands where the Church exists without temporal assistance—much to tempt minds even greater than Montalembert's to consider the severance of Church from State as a superior system; and did not Holy Church herself point to its evils and dangers, they might escape our notice. For us it is well as it is, since it is so that God gives it to us, and when He chooses to give the "second best," we must take it submissively, and work accordingly, never neglecting, however, to pay the due tribute of praise to that which is better. Thus it is that with us, although M. Niels would not be able to understand it immediately, the clergy may accept the help of the laity in a greater degree than in some other lands—for our good, kind God will in these cases give the grace of a peculiar vocation which He withholds where such assistance is unnecessary.

Five years' acquaintance with European journalism, upon whose pages Cardinal Manning stands among prominent figures, had made us familiar with many lovely traits in his character, as well as with the power of his intellect which enables him to be so great a defender of the Church. Certainly not less than his logical eloquence does this unfailing gentleness and loveliness win souls to God, and even the enemies of the Church could cease a moment from their violent abuse of religion to tell with admiration of the manner in which Archbishop Manning was known alike in cottage and manor house, reproving, advising, consoling, entering into the joys and sorrows of all, irrespective of rank or condition. In him the world can behold the perfect fulfilment of a vocation most necessary where the Church is regulated as it seems to please God that it shall be for the present among us who use the English tongue. In other lands, where the temporal affairs of the Church depend only on the State, the clergy are not obliged to mingle so freely with the people, and they may, if they wish, follow all the wise counsels of St. Philip Neri, and retire completely from the world, knowing it only through the misery which it is their vocation to alleviate, speaking to it only through the confessional and the pulpit, or at the bedside of the sick and dying. Free from many of the cares which our system entails, they are at leisure to give themselves to study, to a life of progressive piety, and to devote their energies to devising all manner of means for the salvation of souls, means of guiding more early those already on the road to perfection, and means of attracting those enslaved by the allurements of sinful pleasure to the path of virtue. This last was the system which M. Niels would understand, and it would take an intellect more powerful than even Cardinal Manning's to convince him that there was anything trustworthy in that which is decidedly its opposite.

At half-past one o'clock we at length felt ourselves at liberty to repair to Louise's house, and we walked slowly through the streets of Fayt, slowly over the stony highway leading to Bois d'Haine. Just the day before the Holy Church throughout the earth had said that when the world was growing cold, the Lord Jesus Christ, desiring to inflame our hearts with the fire of His love, had renewed the Sacred Stigmata of the Passion in the body of Blessed Francis and had shown faith in him in various ways the wonderful mysteries of the Cross.—(Roman Missal, September 17.) That very day, in praising the virtues of the seraphic Joseph of Cupertinum, she had declared that God ordained that His only begotten Son should be lifted upon the Cross, so that all things might be drawn unto Himself.—(Roman Missal, Sept. 18.) As the day before had told us to learn the lessons of bearing our afflictions with patience and making the Cross our sure defence, so this day itself bade us raise our minds above all earthly desires, so as to be able to come into the presence of the Court of Heaven. To all this, the events of that Friday at Bois d'Haine were sounding a grand Amen, grander than the most beautiful finale ever composed by Palestrina, Cherubini, or any of the great masters of religious music; and as there are certain sounds in nature that range either too high or too low for the ordinary ear, so there are certain things which, making but slight impressions on the world at large, are yet distinctly audible to the ear of the willing soul, so it was that day that we heard the seeming discords melting into harmony and proclaiming the glory of the Cross of Christ.

Indeed that little cottage, around which expectant groups were gathered on the afternoon of that bright September day, seemed like a sanctuary; for there was that atmosphere of quiet and peace which always rests on the scene of a holy action, and which extends its influence even over the unbeliever. Among those assembled before Louise's door there were many whom we had not as yet seen; for those who had received permission by letter had just arrived on the noonday train. Among these were two German ladies, accompanied by a priest, whom, from his dress and general appearance, we judged to be a personage of no slight importance in his native place. There was also a religieuse of one of the uncloistered orders, and several Belgian clergymen. The others were women of the middle classes, remarkable neither for age nor for any other qualification which one might suppose desirable for admittance to Louise Lateau's cottage.*

Never, even under the influence of the most solemn surroundings, do we lose our individual peculiarities, the stamp of personal identity, and we are never more ourselves than when we

---

* We are repeatedly informed that ladies are no longer admitted to Louise's cottage—no person of the female sex. There were certain hours always, at which only doctors and priests were permitted to come, and others at which persons of every condition could receive permission to enter. From a letter written by the Rev. Joachim Adam, dated Menage, September 28-29, 1877, we quote the following: "I hurried to the house of the ecstatica—there I met several priests; there were also a few nuns present, and a few secular ladies and gentlemen." Again: "Arrived at the house, we noticed a few nuns and some Christian brothers—they all followed us in." (See *Ave Maria*, Nov. 10, 1877.)

are face to face with serious facts; for then we forget the self-possession with which we are accustomed to veil, not control, the operations of our character. At Louise's door there was not that uniformity of action which the American Catholic would expect, but each one followed a different impulse—some withdrew from their companions to wait in silence, perhaps to pray, while others gathered in groups to speak in low tones of their expectations, or else to discuss Cardinal Manning and his friends.

"An Archbishop, that!" exclaimed one of the women; "why, he is dressed quite like a layman, and you say he is a famous prelate! They do strangely in England!"

We looked at Cardinal Manning, who stood at some little distance talking with an English gentleman, beside whom stood a lady who did answer precisely to the description of "exceedingly well-bred." We could not forbear a smile, as we wondered where the good woman had ever seen a layman wearing a closely-buttoned frock coat of such extreme length, and if the gentlemen in Belgium wore black cloth gaiters reaching nearly to the knee, which were such excellent substitutes for the knee-breeches, and black stockings of a certain class of Italian ecclesiastics. To us this costume, far less laymanlike than the street-dress of our own priests, and as near an approach to the clerical street-dress of Rome as would be prudent in the clergy of a country like England, seemed to us a yearning for the true ecclesiastical garb— a sentiment which exists in the heart of every faithful, pious priest, who is condemned to disguise himself in lay apparel.

Having once seen Cardinal Manning's face, who can waste further thought on his garments? His is one of those wonderful countenances where gentleness and purity unite to give that appearance of perpetual youth, which masks the evidences of study and learning from those who see strength of character and traces of deep thought in the ravages made by worldly cares and the turmoil of passion. There is the wisdom of the serpent, the harmlessness of the dove in those bright blue eyes, so expressive of keen penetration and of a charity kindled by the flame of Divine Love, and the fairness of complexion more than Saxon in its perfection, that sparkling countenance, rendering so easy belief in the luminous features of Moses, seemed to tell us that not to Louise alone of all in our day and generation is the Blessed Eucharist drink and meat indeed; for it was an idea more incredible than the miracle which we were about to see, that ordinary nourishment could resolve itself into forms so full of spiritual loveliness. If there was any ignominy in being thrust away from the scene of the miracle, if it was painful to stand and watch the successful, the unpleasantness must have been greatly tempered by being accompanied and supported by so illustrious a personage, and we felt that even we could have endured all patiently had we heard those firm, clear tones telling us:

"Don't go away, I shall stay by you; I will stand with you."

A few moments before two o'clock M. le

Curé arrived with a Franciscan monk, and the gentleman and the two ladies whom our hostess had obliged to submit to the public dinner. As they approached the cottage by the winding road leading from Bois d'Haine, the dress of M. le Curé, cloak, cassock and broad-brimmed hat, as well as the more conspicuous costume of the Franciscan, his worn and faded gown, the olive seed rosary at his side, his hempen girdle and brown cloak and cowl, his bare, sandalled feet, and uncovered head, gave the group a picturesque and religious character, which accorded well with the scene and occasion, and we felt that the presence of a son of St. Francis, a member of that Order to whom the devotion to the Sacred Stigmata is a special legacy, a peculiar right, was singularly appropriate.

M. le Curé addressed all present in a low but distinct voice, saying:

"Ladies and gentlemen, at the very earliest moment that it will be possible to enter I will apprize you of the fact."

He then entered Louise's house, leaving his companions among those in waiting.

One accompaniment of Louise's condition is an incomprehensible feeling of humiliation at being seen by any stranger when she is in her state of stigmatization, which feeling is attributed to a special grace designed by God to prevent spiritual pride, and to be the guardian of her humility. Although she tries to conquer these emotions of what may be termed a miraculous shame, this effort causes her a torture which it is impossible for her to conceal, and the family will not allow this suffering to be inflicted; therefore, it is only during her moments of insensibility that such as we are permitted to see her. Doctors and the higher order of clergy, the family welcome at all hours, because they cherish a lingering hope that some physician or some theologian may reverse the hitherto universal verdict of *non est in naturâ*. The Church not only respects the rights of the household and the family, but she is also their jealous defender, and in a matter like this the pastor may use his influence to procure concessions, but he cannot command anything; therefore, in terming the instant that Louise's ecstasy would render her unconscious of all around her, "as soon as it would be possible to enter," M. Niels referred to the concessions which he has succeeded in obtaining—not to any arbitrary arrangement dependent upon his own whims.

IX.

AT length the eagerly expected moment arrived. M. le Curé opened the door, motioned to the blonde gentleman and the ladies accompanying him to enter, and then giving a quick glance, searching for Mgr. Dumont's friends, he beckoned to our party, at the same time speaking to all, bidding them come in. In spite of M. le Curé's attention, we soon found ourselves jostled to the rear by all the rest, each one of whom betrayed the greatest eagerness. As the second door opened we came into the best room, a sewing room evidently, for there were two sewing machines, before one of which sat Adeline Lateau preparing work. Around the room were scattered several piles of half-finished work, principally the underskirts sold by the establishments of ready-made ladies' wear in France and Belgium. In this room the gentlemen left their hats and canes, and some of the ladies their shawls, and we laid our round hats, merely retaining our veils as more appropriate and less likely to obstruct the vision of others. Adeline acted in all respects as if the famous army of spectres had entered, giving no recognition whatever of our existence, until a lady placing a shawl where perhaps it would inconvenience the family, Adeline indicated by an abrupt gesture where it might be placed.

The doctor came hurriedly into the room to meet us, no longer a gay and careless youth, but a man sobered and aged by all that he had witnessed. As we glanced at his countenance, we saw an awe-struck expression that even the most skeptical could not but ascribe to the holiest influences. Amid the matted locks of hair no longer glossy black, but tangled and drenched by the crowds of thought and by vivid impressions that had passed through his brain, we could discern the threads of silver; it seemed as if eternity had been so near him that it had invested him with a reflection of its own unbeginning age. All his adventurous spirit had died away, and his manner, as he addressed us was as if we, in days remote, had been the companions of a far off childhood, as if we had grown into old age together, and now, on the boundaries of another world, where all the foibles of humanity cease, he wished to tell us of the wonders of that region into which he had been the first to penetrate.

"Oh, madame!" he whispered, as he lead us forward, "it is far more wonderful than all that we are told of her. M. le Curé says that to-day her sufferings have been greater than usual. Just but a moment since she was conversing with us, and now she is perfectly insensible to everything around her."

The kitchen, a tiny place, was next entered, and connecting with it was another little room, perfectly destitute of furniture—a half-window, which was open, admitted light and air. This was Louise's own room, and it was crowded—twenty-one persons, the two doctors not included, having been admitted, and as we were the last to come in we scarcely found space enough to follow the impulse to kneel when we beheld Louise, and we might not have had so much space had it not been for the civility of the doctor's son and of the gentleman with whose party we had dined. Indicating more by gesture than by words where we might place ourselves advantageously, they drew more closely to the wall, whispering softly:

"We can stand behind you very conveniently."

Thus we knelt beside Louise at her left; M. le Curé and the Franciscan were at her right hand, while the others stood just before her, almost touching her garments.

The Stigmatica was poised rather than seated on the edge of a simple straw chair, appearing not really to require its aid in retaining her posture, and her gaze was fixed upward, slightly to the right. All traces of the crown of thorns had disappeared, save a few drops of blood on the left temple, but her hair was still damp, for her sisters had carefully washed her head as soon as the crown had ceased to shed blood. This, however, had failed to remove all the blood stains, and wherever her hair was not hidden by her black cap the red marks faded into pink were distinctly visible. Between the hours of noon and two o'clock, P. M., the blood at that period gradually stopped issuing from all her wounds excepting those in her hands. Evidently her sisters had taken all possible pains to prevent us from seeing the full extent of the miracle—already her feet had been washed and covered with stockings and soft felt shoes, and her simple peasant garb, a plain sacque and skirt of black cashmere was very neatly arranged and carefully cleansed. On the floor, however, lay several pieces of white cotton cloth covered with clear red blood, and upon Louise's lap was spread a similar white kerchief drenched with the blood that was streaming from her uplifted hands. It had been, as the doctor said, a day of unusual suffering for her, and thus the wounds in her hands had not even begun to abate their bleeding. Every sinew in the little hands seemed to be racked with pain, though the entranced expression of the shining countenance told that to this sufferer was vouchsafed that relief which Our Lord on the Cross denied to Himself. The fingers were waxen white and drawn and cramped to the utmost capacity of suffering, and from the wounds that penetrated the palms through and through the red arterial blood flowed or rather sprang in frequent jets. The young doctor fulfilled his mission mechanically; convinced of the supernatural character of these phenomena, he was nevertheless pledged to Dr. Lefebvre to submit everything to the test of science. Once in performing his allotted duties, he turned Louise's hand in such a manner that we were enabled to see clearly the exact shape of the wound. Not round, but rather square, seemingly made by a nail bearing the same proportion to her size as the Holy Nail preserved in the Church of Santa Croce in Gerusalemme does to the traditional stature of Our Lord.

The other doctor made no attempt at science.

Appalled by the miracle, he took his place quietly among the other spectators, in no way differing from them, save that he could say with more positive confidence *non est in naturâ*.

As soon as order had been established in the little room, the rustling of garments and the inaudible whispers were replaced by a profound silence—some recited the Rosary, some moved their lips as they repeated familiar prayers, and all watched. Louise was immovable—her gaze always upwards; sometimes her features wore an almost joyous expression, then again it became intense sadness, mingled with fear and surprise, but never pain; and though the tears once rolled from her eyes, they were the tears of compassion, not of personal suffering. Once she appeared very much startled, and she then fell upon her knees (as one does when meeting in the street the Holy Viaticum, carried openly as it is in Catholic countries). After remaining in this posture a few seconds, she resumed her seat. The manner of motion, or rather the lack of motion, was truly remarkable. She seemed to change her position by a simple act of volition; she was on her knees, she was reseated without appearing to rest for the smallest fraction of a second in the intervening space, or to make the intermediate motions. It would be difficult to find in material language terms adequate to describe this change of place—flying is too sluggish, too unwieldy.

As we knelt beside Louise, we seemed to have left time, and to be dwelling in eternity—so many, so vivid were our impressions; each second was filled to overflowing with ideas that it would take volumes to explain. How much of both doctrine and Scripture became clear to our spiritual vision! Isaac bearing his burden along the slopes of Moriah, Jephte's daughter and the Sacrifice of Calvary with its awful darkening of the sun and its last fearful *Consummatum est!* How often, in closing the pages of the Sacred Volume, had we been grateful to the kind cautions of the Church, when she prevents us from exercising our own weak, erring judgment upon the inscrutable ways of God, and from using our one-sided, circumscribed conceptions to interpret the actions of the Infinite and All-knowing. The Spirit of the Lord came upon Jephte, and he made a vow unto the Lord, (Judges xi, 29–30).* Dare we impute rashness to that which was the fruit of inspiration, and yet did not that vow involve the horrible crime of human sacrifice? How grateful we had been, that we were placed in this world to effect our salvation, and not to give decisions on the actions of our Creator! How we had thanked God that He only asked us to know, love, and serve Him, without requiring of us that we should understand Him! Now, beside Louise how easy was the solution of many wearying problems!

Error in one sense is twofold; it consists of distortions of truth and negations of necessary principles, and the most harmful of all its distortions, the most ingenious device that Satan has ever invented to bring contempt upon the mystery of Redemption, is the manner in which idolatry

---

*See the commentary on verse 31 of this Chapter—Douay Bible.

deals with human sacrifice. Modern error adheres strictly to the system of negations, while idolatry consists of a series of frightful misapplications and usurpations. Thus the human blood shed to appease Baal, Moloch or Woden, or that crimsoned the hundred steps of the Mexican teocalis, or which flowed so freely in honor of the false deities of civilized, intellectual, but pagan Rome, or that to-day reddens the sands of Southern Africa, is but a terrible misinterpretation of the sublime principles involved in Redemption and salvation; ideas of which will always be found implanted in the human heart; those principles which were enunciated by the Royal Prophet when he declared that a sacrifice to God was an afflicted spirit.

How human affliction can be an agreeable offering to our Heavenly Father, is often a difficult matter for a finite brain to comprehend, but although God does not see fit to explain this subject to us in all its bearings, still from time to time He brings forth some part thereof in such striking relief, shedding such clear and brilliant light upon it, that belief in the whole becomes an easy possibility to those not too blinded by sin; for the well-known effect of sin is to make us misunderstand revelation and hate God. It is hating God to hate that which He has revealed of Himself, and we cannot escape this imputation by loving a God whom we have invested with attributes more agreeable to our sin-degraded nature. If the judgments of God, the requirements of revealed religion appear harsh and cruel to you, examine well the record of your conscience, and try to cancel the guilt of that unrepented sin which is blinding and trammeling your soul. If we wish to seek one of the many examples of the manner in which God has enveloped sorrow with a peculiar halo, let us consider the effect of suffering on the human soul, and even upon the human features; how many become gentle, saintly, and beautiful under its holy influence! Grace is often neglected, it is true, and some do allow their hearts to grow bitter under affliction, and their faces to assume an habitual expression of hopeless weariness, but in general those who meet death with that perennial youth which they have carried into old age, are the ones upon whom the Hand of the Lord has rested the most heavily.

When we view human sacrifice in its true light, the light afforded by the history of Christianity, we see that it must be accomplished very differently from the requirements of the diabolical rites of paganism. The holocaust must be a self-oblation, and as God does not wish that our hearts should be torn by physical force from the yet living body, the victim must await His will. When holy Kings and Bishops in times of pestilence or famine have offered their lives for those of their people, there was no sacrificial knife, no fire kindled by human hands; for the same Lord who has said " Vengeance is Mine" will also, in the words of Abraham, find the victim and the holocaust, and He will send down the fire from Heaven upon the acceptable sacrifice. Whether this fire shall come in the form of swift and violent death, or long, lingering, painful disease, whether the heart shall be afflicted by losses and bereavements, or the body receive the very marks and endure the sufferings of the Passion of our Lord, it is not for man to demand, nor for human power to put anything of all this into execution.

And we were in the presence of one of these acceptable victims, before one of whom it might be said that God had laid upon her the burden of our sins—one who was suffering that the glory of God might be made manifest in her; and as all these ideas rolled rapidly through our minds, we never once thought that in our own native land we would ever hear from the lips of those calling themselves sincere Catholcis, any expressions of wonder concerning the end and object of these sufferings. One of the many changing forms of general heresy declares that it is blasphemous to suppose that the sufferings of a being purely human can be, in any manner, rendered available to eternal salvation either for himself or for others, because the sufferings of Christ were both necessary and all-sufficient. Necessary they were, and all-sufficient they might have been, had not God willed otherwise; for in His eternal wisdom He has decreed that we ourselves shall win the prize, although the means of earning it, as well as the prize itself, come from Him. He allows us, He wishes us to go to Him of our own free will, by our own exertion; in the words of St. Augustine, "God who made you without you, will not save you without you;" and not only this, but God also allows us, wishes us to assist one another. In accordance with this, the Church teaches—and we must listen to her voice, and not allow ourselves to be infected with the leaven of the errors rampant around us—that the sufferings of Christ opened Heaven to those who *co-operate* with the graces His Passion obtained for mankind; that His Precious Blood hallows all our good deeds, all our penitential acts, all our patient endurance of pain and sorrow, so that they become acceptable offerings to God for ourselves and for our neighbor.

Without Its all-sanctifying influence, no good deeds, no penance, no endurance would be of any avail before God, but through Its redeeming powers we are entitled to present ourselves and our own meritorious acts before the throne of God, and these works may plead not only for ourselves, but, if we have had the happiness to do more than win our place in Heaven, we may thereby obtain graces for others. In confirmation of this consoling doctrine, rises up the history of the establishment of Christianity. Had God willed that the Passion of Our Lord should found and foster the Church without the co-operation of human suffering, there would have been no need for the blood of martyrs to prepare the soil of every land for the planting of the Gospel. Even in the light of mere human reason, the belief of the Catholic Church is more consistent with the conditions that surround us, to agree with the ideas condemned by the Church, man ought to have been restored by the Redemption to the primitive state of Adam, to enjoy the same freedom from original sin and all its pains and penalties, pain and affliction included, but these remain with man, and those who question the utility of Louise's sufferings ought also to ask, why do these ills continue?—for what good?

Admitting, as every Christian must, the justice of the punishment of original sin—and the most ordinary intellect can understand, if it only will, that since God intended to justify the whole human race in consequence of one man's obedience, it is but proper that the results of Adam's fall should be imposed upon all mankind—it then becomes easy of comprehension why some should be able to suffer for sins in which they had no part. Since we suffer the penalties of transmitted sin which we did not personally commit, why should we not be capable of performing expiation for any sin, no matter where committed, no matter who the offender may be? When the innocent thus suffer for the guilty, vengeance becomes mercy; for thereby the sinner obtains grace sufficient for repentance and for a reunion with the merits of the Precious Blood. Admitting the doctrine of mutual expiation under the law of the Precious Blood of Our Lord Jesus Christ, it is no longer difficult to understand how it is that God has a right to claim not only a certain number of prayers and good works from a city, province or country, but also a certain amount of repentance and expiation, and that if these four expressions of homage and fealty are neglected by one portion of the community, the faithful must redouble their efforts, and prevent this spiritual tribute from being in the least diminished, and as, although He never really forces, God often assists man in his efforts to serve Him, so He Himself in His infinite wisdom often selects among the willing, suitable victims of an expiation neglected by the sinner himself.

For those who really believe all, all that the Church teaches, what a glorious world of consoling thought concerning sorrow and pain does she spread before the eyes of the soul! Then we are no longer isolated identities living each for himself; our trials, our sufferings are no longer fruitless, terminating in ourselves, and dying with us, but they are a bond between us and the whole human family. Then we behold how all Christians are united in cancelling the common debt incurred by original sin, the debt which rests equally on us all, and yet the penalties of which are laid more heavily on souls most fortified by grace, just as the work of a household is seldom equally divided, the stronger fulfilling the tasks of the weaker.

Invalids, who see yourselves condemned to years of hopeless pain and helpless dependence on others, you are the strong, you are doing the noblest work, performing the most difficult task, doing for those who wait on your bodily weakness that which perhaps they are incapable of doing for themselves, winning for them graces from which perhaps they have been so far removed that they did not even feel the need of them. How these thoughts ennoble pain! What a source of endless consolation, and of patience, and of fortitude! You watch the busy steps of the rest of your family as they are engaged in household duties, but you know that, although chained to your bed, you are not idle, that your sufferings are all your own and more precious than gold and silver, for with them you may purchase graces and blessings without number for those upon whom you are apparently but a worthless burden. Perhaps that same temporal happiness and complete prosperity which your sufferings seem to mar, depend upon just this affliction; perhaps God has chosen you as the expiation of that portion of the debt of inherited sin resting on your family, thereby making you the shield to defend your dear ones from sorrow and disappointment.

Mothers, who see your little infants washed by baptism from every stain of aught that could render them displeasing to God, struggling with pain which you cannot assuage, dying in the midst of torture more keen than that inflicted by Herod's cruel soldiery, what meagre consolation you find in the truisms which tell you " that it is all done in love," " all the work of a merciful Father," without giving you a single ray of light by which your tearstained eyes might see this love and mercy, but when our tender Mother the Church assumes the task of condolence she utters no trite platitudes, but turning like a careful householder to her inexhaustible treasurehouse, the Sacred Scriptures, she brings forth the martyrdom of the Holy Innocents, and, showing the glorious fruits of their death she bids you see the like beautiful results of the sufferings of your little ones. As these blessed infants by their violent end not only received higher places in the dwellings of everlasting joy, but also thereby atoned for the sin of inhospitality towards the Holy Family, and obtained that the blessing of a constant and perfect communion with the Church of Christ, already granted to Bethlehem by being the birth-place of the Redeemer, should be confirmed and continued to the end of time, so yours, having through their sickness and pain within a short space fulfilled all the suffering and woe of a long life without any of its sin, (Wisdom iv. 13) not only arrive at their destined places in heaven, but also through their innocence and suffering atone for the faults of the family, and obtain for their parents, their brothers and their sisters priceless blessings without number.* It is by meditations such as these that the Church endeavors to teach resignation, only resignation, for to literally turn mourning into rejoicing would frustrate the holy aim of affliction, but it is only because meditation can never equal revelation that to be resigned is the sole result of these consoling ideas. Had the vast amount of grace, procured for generation unto generation, been placed by revelation before your predeces-

---

* "Ce petit enfant qui souffre est peut-être une victime expiatrice pour les fautes qui pèsent sur toute une famille .... au lieu de venger les droits de la justice sur tout cette famille coupable, si Dieu se contente d'une innocente victime pour epargner les autres: n'est-ce point de sa part, une acte de la misericorde? .... si grâce à ce sacrifice cet enfant comme un ange du ciel doit retrouver plus tard dans le bonheur et dans la gloire, le pere et la mere dont il aura été comme le sauveur, ne sera-ce-point pour tous une genereuse et magnifique compensation?"—*Souffrances et Consolations par M. l'Abbé A. Riche, prêtre de la Congregation de St. Sulpice, Paris.*

sors in woe, the mothers of Bethlehem, the voice of lamentation heard in Rama would have been hushed by an ecstasy of joy.

When we find ourselves bound by what the world terms inexorable fate, but which Christians know as Divine Providence, to a round of duties which weary us with their incessant sameness, dishearten us by their lack of importance, may we not find relief in the thought that while we are patiently fulfilling these seemingly trivial tasks, we are perhaps storing up more graces than our spiritual needs demand, thus rendering ourselves capable of assisting some weary soul somewhere on the surface of the earth, perhaps, if even ever so little, we are helping to strengthen the heart of the missionary in savage lands, or we may be gaining the final grace necessary for the following of some holy vocation. When eternity shall annihilate time and space, perhaps one of the sweet surprises will be to find how closely we have been united with those who dwell in the uttermost parts of the earth.

Sufferings like Louise's, ah! those are a perpetual fountain of grace, springing up before the throne of God, and falling in refreshing showers upon the parched world! For what good? Let not those ask who have received spiritual favors beyond that which they have sought to merit. Why have so many of those dear to you entered the Church of Christ? Why has the favor of a death-bed repentance been so often unexpectedly granted to members of your family after perhaps years of an un-Christian life on their part? Is it owing to your midnight vigils, your penances? Is it because you have spent hours before the Blessed Sacrament seeking for mercy from the morning watch even until night? You pursued not one of these practices; ask yourselves then if these graces are not the work of some of those willing victims of reparation, of those who unselfishly, with no other thought than the love of God, offer up without ceasing all their actions, all their sufferings for the conversion of sinners, not caring who these sinners may be, or to what nation they may belong, only asking that the offence to God may cease, only that souls ransomed by the Precious Blood of Christ may not become the prey of the most Wicked One.

We had not been a long time in Louise's room, when the shrill shriek of an engine whistle aroused us from our meditations, and the heavy rumbling of a train laden with iron-ore shook the cottage to its very foundations. Everyone among us, excepting Louise, gave a start of surprise; she remained immovable, not a muscle relaxed, not a feature changed expression, there was not even the rigidness of self-control—too evidently, Louise was totally insensible to the exterior world.

Shortly after this, the priests began to read aloud the canonical office of the day and hour, in which they were joined by the two students from Rome. The low ceiling gave a peculiar resonance to their powerful voices, and the surrounding circumstances an additional solemnity to the inspirations of the Holy Ghost. They must have all been well practiced in reading the canonical office in chorus, for they repeated it in perfect unison, in spite of marked differences in the method of pronouncing Latin—the Belgians transposing the sounds of the vowels, the Germans adhering strictly to the hard g, while the Roman students steadily persevered in the observance of every rule of the Italian school of pronunciation. To us it seemed like a type of the manner in which the Church can blend all nations, all rites, into one harmonious whole. As in all the cathedrals and in many of the other churches of Europe, the canonical hours are either read or chanted daily, it becomes a necessity for the laity to learn to carry out their individual private devotions, undisturbed by the repetition of these psalms and lessons—therefore, all the ladies still held their rosaries in their hands, and they might have continued to recite this form of prayer, had not their attention been attracted by the extraordinary effect of the psalms and antiphons on Louise. Even without understanding the language in which these were read, their general tenor might have been gathered from the various expressions of awe, joy, sadness or compassion that flitted across her countenance, and from these changes of expression directors of choirs would learn the shade of feeling with which each verse of these psalms should be chanted. These variations of feature did not seem so much a voluntary contraction of any particular set of muscles, as they appeared the effect of causes purely external; they were flashes of spiritual light irradiating her features, or withdrawing to leave them in shadow, just as the sun, having rested on the ripples of water, and having turned every drop to molten silver, retreats behind a cloud and leaves the stream to its own glassy dullness.

"He shall drink of the torrent in the way," (Ps. cix, 8). How eagerly, wistfully, sadly, she gazed upward! Was it given to her to see in one swift vision the sad foliage of Gethsemani, waving in the light of the Easter moon, the glare of torchlight revealing the traitorous kiss of Judas; Cedron, rolling in all its spring-tide violence over its stony bed amid the silent tombs of the Valley of Josaphat? Did she see Our Lord buffetted by the muddy waters as the executioners fling Him over the bridge of torture into "the torrent in the way?"* If so, this vision was quickly effaced by the jubilant triumph of the eternal glory celebrated in the doxology. Did the psalm speak of the fear of the Lord, the shadow of an inexpressible awe rested on her face; did it promise an everlasting recompense to the just, a joyous smile seemed to part her lips; did it tell how beyond all praise is the exceeding glory of the Most Holy Trinity, her uplifted countenance reflected the bliss of the Seraphim, and always, as each psalm drew to its close did she anxiously await the *Gloria Patri*, which we could see greeted her ear like a strain of glorious exultant music.

He hath had regard for the humility of His handmaid; He that is mighty hath done great things to me, and holy is His Name. So sang centuries ago in the hill-country of Judea a

---

* See the visions of Catherine Emmerich.

daughter of the royal house of David, the Virgin Mother of God, but Louise Lateau might well listen with joyful assent as the voice of the Church repeated these words beneath the lowly roof of her little cottage; for the same God who looked with complacence on the humility of her who was not only royal, but immaculate, had also loved the humility of the peasant maid, and, placing her, as it were, beneath the Cross of her Redeemer beside His Blessed Mother, He has done great things to her, and holy is His Name.

The voices of the readers rose and fell; now it was the clear high tones of the youths which predominated, then came in the deep voices of the older priests; the psalms began to refer more and more distinctly to the Passion of Christ, mingling the darkness of Calvary with the triumph of the Resurrection and the Ascension, in the sublime manner peculiar to these royal prophecies, and the flashes of expression on Louise's face changed their character still more rapidly, while the blood flowed with still greater violence from her hands. As the beginning of the Miserere reached our ears, we beheld Louise on her knees, to which position she had arrived by her own inexplicable method of motion; she remained kneeling during the first five verses of that grand appeal for mercy—and for whom was she imploring this mercy? Not for herself alone, for wherein could she have ever seriously offended God? Was it not for the world of sinners that she made her appeal? The uplifted hands of Moses were acceptable without those holy marks which Christ loved so well that, retaining them in His glorified Body, He carried them with Him to the Right Hand of the Father. What oceans of grace hands, thus marked with the seal of the Lamb, must draw down upon those in whose behalf they are raised!

"A sacrifice to God is an afflicted spirit: a contrite and humble heart, O God, Thou wilt not despise."—(Ps. l. 19.) "Burnt-offering and sin-offering Thou didst not require: then said I, Behold I come."—(Ps. xxxix. 7.) These were the words that seemed to arouse most fully the spirit of expiation, especially the last quoted verse. More rapidly than our minds could do it did her face translate the meaning of each line, and at the end of the verse she bent yet more forward, and the red stream burst afresh from the stigmata of her hands, an echo, a response to " Behold, I come."

As we watched eagerly this living commentary, who was interpreting Scripture for us, not only more clearly than any verbal or printed explanation could do, but who also caused us to see in certain passages a meaning precisely opposite to that which we had without much reflection ascribed to them, our attention was attracted to one whose presence we had not at first remarked. Rosine Lateau, her eyes gleaming with an unearthly displeasure, sat in the corner behind her sister engaged in sewing, her feet resting on the highest round of Louise's chair, and being occasionally elevated as high as its seat. The door partially screened many of us from her view, but frequently she paused in her work to glance angrily around the room, even bending forward, so that she might not only see everyone of its occupants, but that she also might let us perceive how very unwelcome we all were. Certain analogies between her angry manner towards us who were assembled in prayer around her suffering sister, and the conduct of the infuriated mob with regard to the faithful few who gathered around Our Lord on Mt. Calvary, would creep into our minds every time that we were forced to observe the but half smothered rage visible in those terrible black eyes.

If we thought of those without, who not able to see that which we saw, personated as it were those "standing afar off," it was to regret for them that they had not accepted M. Niel's final offer. To be present, were it only for fifteen minutes at the portion of the day's events embraced in this hour of ecstasy, would be a greater favor than it would be possible for a person who has not seen this part of Louise's miraculous state to imagine. That which ordinary individuals are permitted to see is a very small part when considered in relation to the whole, but when compared with the merely natural events of life it is a very great deal; were Louise's present condition restricted to that which takes place within this one hour, were the wonders of her life to consist but of the events which we witnessed, she would still be worthy of the notice of the whole world. That one hour is an ample proof of the verity of all that of which we are told, and it sets the seal of truth on every assertion made by Louise's biographers.

Whenever our attention was turned for a second from Louise to the other occupants of the room, seeing the marked alteration in the doctor caused us to recollect with peculiar vividness one of the most beautiful passages in Henri Lasserre's work on Notre Dame de Lourdes, that famous remark of the Basque peasant who stood amidst a crowd that was watching Bernardette during one of the apparitions of Our Lady of Lourdes.

"In beholding Bernardette," said he, "who

can doubt that the Blessed Virgin is present? In my native valley it is many hours after sunrise before we are able to see the sun itself, so high are our mountains, but there is one lofty peak west of our hamlet which catches the very first rays of the rising sun, and when we see its snow-capped summit brilliant with rosy tints, who among us could deny the existence and the presence of the sun? And so it is with us and this child, while we are in the valley, she on the mountain top of celestial favors has her countenance illuminated by the glory of another world."

How wonderfully the reflection of that which is, after all, the mere shadow of the Passion, appeared in the manner and expression of this young man who, not twenty-four hours before, had betrayed all the thoughtless though harmless gaiety of youth, and now—let the "Come, follow Me," be whispered ever so softly, at the first syllable of the invitation he would have been ready to turn his back on all the fleeting pleasure of the world to enter upon the most severe monastic life. Of his subsequent conduct we can of course know nothing, for our acquaintance ended in Louise's room; but of this we are sure, that if he has remained in the ordinary path of Christian life, it is because such is the vocation assigned him by God, and as Our Father in Heaven also loves with an infinite love those whom He has appointed to form by remaining in the world the body of the faithful, He showers, too, upon them grace in infinite abundance. If it had been so astonishing to watch the effect of the whole course of this miracle upon the doctor, how glorious a privilege would it have been to see the same causes acting upon Cardinal Manning, to watch *his* countenance reflecting the glory of the wonderful works of God!

The office was finished, the voices of the readers were silent, and for a few minutes Louise was not subjected to any exterior influence; she was seated in the same position in which we found her, her gaze fixed upwards, her senses closed to our material world; suddenly she was on her knees, perfectly straight and rigid, but at the same time inclining her whole person forward, so as to bring her head much in advance of her knees and thus she remained for two or three minutes. By the laws of gravitation this posture is impossible to ordinary men and women, as those accustomed to kneeling can testify, and practised gymnasts who have seen Louise during her ecstacy, have declared that according to natural laws no amount of training can enable any one to retain this position longer than a second. In assuming it she had precipitated herself into the midst of the opposite group, consisting of the two ladies whom we had met at the hotel, the German priest, and his two friends. The first mentioned drew back, perhaps former experience had taught the lady in mourning to do so, but the Germans remained in the same place, their countenances expressing how great an honor they esteemed this close proximity. Suddenly a shrill, angry voice broke the solemn silence.

"M. le Curé, they have taken some of her

blood!" cried Rosine, and she added, with a look of triumphant superiority, "Here, that can't be done."

M. Niels, with one of his own inimitable looks of non-committal, began a seemingly vigilant search, but it was remarkably impossible for him to discover the offender.

"He did; I saw him; that one there!" exclaimed Rosine, indicating the German priest by a rude, angry gesture.

"Let me see your handkerchief." said M. Niels, in the mildest of tones.

As the German priest drew it forth, we understood why when we first entered we had been told to keep our handkerchiefs in our pockets.

"It is all right, all right," whispered M. Niels in Flemish, a dialect sufficiently resembling German for the priest to comprehend, but which is not spoken by the peasantry of Bois d'Haine who use a corruption of French. Rosine had no alternative; she was obliged to accept M. Niels' act as decisive, and she resumed her sewing, comparing the effect of two different styles of trimming, while Louise again placed herself on the chair. That season some lady of Brussels purchased an underskirt for ten francs, never knowing its peculiar value.

This scene is always recalled to our minds whenever we hear American Catholics criticising the pious customs of older nations, speaking contemptuously of practices that have had not only the permission, but also the approval, the sanction of everyone who has sat upon the Chair of Peter. When we have heard these persons boasting that this or that " can never be done here," we make the same comparison between them and the objects of their scorn, as we then did between the illiterate peasant woman and the elegant, highly educated, perhaps even learned gentleman whom she called " That one there."

As soon as this little difficulty had been settled to the satisfaction of all, excepting Rosine, M. le Curé bade us observe how Louise was affected by the contact of blessed objects, and we did see that any article, no matter how it might refer to religion, was unnoticed by her, unless it had been previously blessed. Whatever was blessed caused her countenance to be illuminated by the smile already described, and she would endeavor to grasp an object to which she had exhibited the utmost indifference before it had received a blessing, which had been given without her knowledge. However, this phase of her condition was not shown to us in a manner perfectly satisfactory, but Louise had endured so much during the morning hours that it was not deemed advisable to make many experiments, as it is often very painful to her when the regular course of her visions is interrupted. The reader will readily conceive that, to experiment freely would be irreverent, every pious heart would shrink from treating Louise just like a person under mesmeric influence, upon whom one may play any trick suggested by their love of the marvelous.

The prayers of the Church are always a source of pleasure to Louise when she is in this condition, so M. le Curé asked the German priest to repeat either the Lord's Prayer or the "Hail Mary."

"You will see," said he, "that although it will be in his own language, she will understand, though she does not know either German or Flemish."

The German priest recited the Lord's Prayer, and the effect was similar to that produced by the psalms of the Office—each one of the seven petitions altered her expression, and at the close she bowed her head almost before the priest said " Amen."

"Will you read the prayer in honor of the Five Wounds?" said M. le Curé to the Franciscan.

The monk opened his breviary, and from a sheet of letter paper lying between its pages he read aloud in Latin a prayer to the Five Wounds of Our Lord, to the recital of which many indulgences are attached. At this Louise was again on her knees, her expression according completely with the spirit of the prayer.

When it was concluded, she resumed her seat, and, after a few moments, M. le Curé consulted his watch, remarking to the Franciscan that it was nearly three o'clock. Rather by signs than by words, he then asked one of the Belgian priests to say the Confiteor; this was the second time that it had been repeated during that hour, but the Confiteor of the Complin had not been especially noticed by Louise; for this one she knelt, filled apparently with the sentiments of the deepest contrition. We knew that the Papal blessing and the absolution of the hour of death is read over Louise every Friday afternoon by a priest having the authority from Rome, and we surmised that as the Confiteor is the preliminary to the Papal benediction, that these were about to be read; nor were we mistaken. The Franciscan again opened his book and began the Latin formula of the blessing and absolution. There was no room to stand before Louise, so he retained his place beside M. le Curé; she remained on her knees, her face evincing the most childlike delight at every proposition contained in the blessing. The absolution began, and her joy seemed to know no bounds when she heard herself released from all the penalties of her sins—those which she had committed through ignorance, as well as those of which she was conscious. As the monk uttered the words, "In virtue of the authority vested in me by the Holy See, I absolve thee," etc., we saw that Louise, without rising from her knees, had altered her position swiftly, so as to kneel at his feet; surprise choked his speech, and his uplifted hand trembled as he made the sign of the Cross over Louise's head.

After all that we had seen, there did not remain the slightest doubt in our minds as to the fact that Louise would, while in this ecstasy, understand the prayers of the Church, no matter in what language they were repeated. Those who have not witnessed this remarkable exemplification of the manner in which the discords of Babel are resolved into harmony in the other world, might be inclined to think that, perhaps, her ear had been accustomed to the sounds contained in those prayers which are always recited in her cottage on Friday, but by our own experience we are convinced that it would require a degree of familiarity with Latin impossible for one otherwise without education to be able, by means purely natural, to correspond so simultaneously, so accurately with what is read in that tongue. The Canonical Office, as every Catholic who takes an interest in the liturgy of the Church knows, is so variable that it would be extremely difficult for her to learn every portion of it so as to understand—as she evidently does—every verse of the psalms, every line of the antiphons. Naturally, we had been obliged, during our sojourn in different lands, to accommodate our ear to various methods of pronouncing Latin, but often, had it not been for the assistance given us by Louise's varying expression, we could not have overcome the difficulties, the confusion, occasioned by the mixture of the different accents.

"Will you stand aside as much as possible?" whispered M. Niels to those who were opposite Louise. "When it is three o'clock she will fall on the floor, you know, and you must leave her sufficient space."

He was instantly obeyed, and we all awaited the culminating point in deep silence. With all the fleetness of the six wings of the Seraphim Louise flew from her chair forward, downward, her arms outstretched as if to greet an invisible crucifix. All that which in the life of St. Joseph of Cupertinum appears so unreal, so incredible to the American Catholic, became to us in that moment living facts. So absorbed were we in wonder that we scarcely noticed Rosine's haste to secure the cloths covered with her sister's blood, hardly reflected upon what the enemies of the Church would style the incongruity of the ignorant preventing the educated and the learned from practising relic-worship. Our meditations were first interrupted by the anxiety which M. Niels betrayed; we do not know if it has been foretold to Louise that there will be a Friday on which she will complete the similarity between her sufferings and those of Our Lord by dying on her invisible Cross; the fact of the absolution being read for her would point that way, and no less so the fear exhibited by her pastor.

"Who has the correct time?" said he in a voice too full of agitation to be anything but a choked whisper.

"We have adjusted our watches from the time at the University of Louvain," replied several, among them the two doctors, "and it lacks several minutes of three o'clock."

"Doctor, will you see if her feet are crossed?" said M. le Curé.

When Louise prostrated herself at full length her garments had clung closely to her figure in a perfectly graceful, modest manner, and now her feet were almost entirely concealed from view. Kneeling down and bending over, the doctor ascertained that they were one or two inches apart instead of being crossed as they are at the moment of completing the crucifixion.

"Will some one say the Lord's Prayer? Doctor watch if her face betrays any recognition of the words," said M. Niels.

The doctor changed his position, and kneeling at her head, he felt her wrist.

"Her pulse is beating," he remarked.

One of the priests repeated the Lord's Prayer, Louise raised her forehead from the floor at the very first syllable, and as we heard "Amen," we could all see that she inclined her head.

"She heard it, M. le Curé! she heard it!" said the doctor. "I read it in her face."

The older doctor still held his watch in his hand and just as we saw that it was at length three o'clock Louise's feet drew together and crossed like those of a crucifix; her arms became more outstretched, although they curved decidedly, the left arm much more than the right, as if strained downward by her weight, while her head drooped towards her right side.

All was finished, and we knelt a few moments in silence and prayer, while Rosine stood beside her sister, her eyes full of a mute entreaty that we would now leave them alone with their great misfortune.

"Perhaps," said M. Niels, "it will be just as well to go now, there have been some occasions on which Louise has returned to consciousness after being in this position but a few moments, and you don't know how it would distress her to see you all here. Generally she remains as you see her there until after four o'clock; she then spends some time between kneeling and sitting, just as you have seen, and by five o'clock all is past, her wounds are healed, she is restored to consciousness, she is able to resume her duties, and by to-morrow she will be in as good health as any one of us, much stronger and better than some of you."

We arose and passed into the sewing-room, where we found Adeline employed as we had left her; on seeing us she laid aside her work, and going to the outside door she opened it and held it slightly ajar, so that one person at a time could go out; this precaution was to prevent those who were standing outdoors from entering. As we replaced our bonnets we remarked that all the Germans, the ladies as well as the priest, had secured some drops of Louise's blood on fine cambric handkerchiefs—a devout act which, as we have seen, met with Rosine's profound disapprobation. If we ourselves had not desired to imitate this party it was not because we shared in Rosine's un-Catholic sentiments, it was reverence that so impelled us, not either indifference or contempt. It would be difficult to honor too highly blood issuing from the counterparts of the wounds received by Christ for our salvation, blood whose sole nourishment is the Blessed Eucharist.

While we were passing out one by one through the narrow aperture left by Adeline, an elderly lady who had been waiting on the outside attempted to enter, apparently not knowing that this was not permitted. Adeline thrust her back with a violence that caused the old lady to totter and to turn pale; then wishing to close the door, Adeline accelerated the movements of the one about to go out by a push that was gentle only by comparison, and the arm that pens these lines bore for many a day in black and blue the marks of that gentle push. The door was then shut with a vehemence not to be expressed otherwise than by the word slam, and had it not been for the solemn scene through which the majority of those who saw the whole of this rude conduct had just passed, indignant exclamations would have been general; as it was, the holy influences under which we had been, enabled us to conquer anger and to feel only a slight degree of amusement, expressed by a universal smile—a ghastly one it was. When the door was again opened, M. Niels himself acted the porter, and as the last person came out the English lady stepped forward to ask him a question, but hardly had she said " M. le Curé," when he showed by an abrupt gesture that he had nothing to say to her, at least not there, and the door of Louise's cottage was once more closed.

X.

WHEN our little party was again together, we hastened, by a common impulse, to the church of Bois d'Haine, to find in the tranquillizing presence of the Blessed Sacrament means of arranging the confused ideas filling our over-wrought minds, and so we parted from those who had been our companions during the most remarkable experience of our lives—each one going forward to meet the Cross, whose weight would be the better endured through the graces which the earnest contemplation of Our Lord's Passion had procured, the more cheerfully borne because of the recollection of the sufferings that day witnessed. For we believe that all those who are permitted by Divine Providence to see Louise, are those whom affliction awaits; one who has written her life in a strain of the most touching piety, left her presence to learn of the sudden death of a much loved son; Father Majunke, whose account of Louise had guided our footsteps to her cottage door, when he returned to his native land, after having visited Louise, was cast into prison, there to spend weeks and months; and when we regained the shores of America, we found our Cross all-prepared for us. Thanks to the lovely legends of the Franciscan Order, which are always singing the praises of poverty in jubilant strains; thanks to a realizing sense of the poverty of the Holy Family, and of its thoroughly voluntary nature, which one is forced to attain in Palestine—we no longer considered the lack of riches in the light of anything save freedom from a very great responsibility. Sickness and pain are familiar acquaintances with the generality of mortals, and it is comparatively easy to learn patient endurance with regard to them, but when we have learned to disregard these, God knows how to find a cross that will be really a cross; for He knows our vulnerable places, and it is there that He tries us in order to prove to us our weakness, and it is always well for us to discover where we are feeble. Now, when our burdens grow very wearisome, we call to mind all our companions of that hour, and we are certain that wherever they may be, unless death has released them from earth, and purgatory delivered their souls all cleansed from the rust of sin into paradise, that they are bearing a heavy cross all the more courageously because of Louise, and we feel that we are still united with them around her, still receiving the lessons which her presence imparted to us.

What practical instruction did we receive from seeing her? Had that question been asked as we left her cottage, we would not have known how to reply. The knowledge obtained by the direct operations of grace differs in countless ways from that which we gain by mere mental effort; acquired information is at first exceedingly vivid and we rejoice in its possession, but when it has been laid away in the storehouse of the mind, it loses its first vigor;

and although we are rarely conscious of the progress of its decay, we find in the moment of need that the knowledge on which we relied has ceased to be available. The instructions of grace are given far otherwise; when we receive them, we are for the most part unconscious of the communication—at best, there is nothing in our minds but a confused murmur like the sighing of the summer wind, or like the sound of distant waves dashing against a rock-bound coast; but as time rolls on, as the day of need approaches, grace-given knowledge becomes more and more defined, and by it we are enabled to accomplish the duties presented to us.

Of that which we learned from Louise we can now enumerate three distinct lessons; perhaps as the years go by others may develop themselves. Although we had never been among those who condemn pilgrimage so freely, without pausing to reflect that the Church gives her best indulgences to this devotion, we had often been at a loss to find many arguments in favor of this custom. We had a vague idea that it would be very wilful and very disobedient to quote the words of even the holiest of men against the advice of an infallible Church, or for Catholics of all countries and all ages to appropriate to themselves a counsel given only to one century or to one province. We had quietly accepted the fact that God and the Church wish to reform the vices of this age by means of pilgrimage, and now at Bois d'Haine it seemed to please the Almighty to give us an insight into the manner by which pilgrimage will work this reform. By becoming a pilgrim you show a willingness to take up your cross, and an accepted pilgrimage, so the guardians of the Holy Sepulchre tell us, is always marked by trials and contradictions which often continue even after the devout act is accomplished. That what involves Heaven-sent crosses can take away from holiness seems incredible, does it not? If we consider that self-knowledge is another grace which is the gift of shrines to impart, we may discover in this fact the origin of the idea that to visit a sanctuary of renown is more liable to retard our spiritual progress than to advance us on the road of Christian perfection. Often while we ought to be still under the sacred influence of these hallowed spots, or even while we are still resting in their very shadow, we are guilty of faults of which we deemed ourselves incapable, and we thus discover what we really are—returning home not less holy than we left, but having learned that we are far less holy than we imagined ourselves to have been. It is useless to say that we can obtain just the same graces by remaining at home—that is impossible; we may gain others which will be all-sufficient for the exigences of our souls; for those graces which fill the atmosphere of shrines may not be necessary for us; if they were God would give us the opportunity of obtaining them, and this opportunity we would be obliged to embrace or else incur the penalty of the imputation of having neglected a Divine gift. Ought we, if we wish to obtain the full benefit of graces placed within our reach, to speak disparagingly of those which are beyond our power to acquire? Some may say that the Church does give just the same graces to those who never visit holy places, quoting in support of this the indulgences attached to the devotion of the Way of the Cross, but if we recall the first institution of this pious custom we will remember that the Church bestowed these indulgencies in consideration of those who, having neither means nor opportunity, have yet an ardent desire to visit the scenes of Our Lord's Passion. It cannot be repeated too often that it is by means of frequent pilgrimages that the Christians of this century are to be purified from the evils which are corrupting all classes, and here the Catholics of the United States cannot enroll themselves among the exceptional cases, for God has inspired some of His servants to erect in our midst, within the reach of a vast multitude, a sanctuary of pilgrimage* dedicated to that devotion, which embraces all

---

* The pilgrimage church of Our Lady of the Sacred Heart, at Notre Dame, Indiana.

the mysteries of religion, by commemorating the Love that prompted the Incarnation and the Redemption, and by honoring the sweet influence of Mary over this Divine Love.

There are sinners all around us, and when we read the lives of those who have died martyrs while carrying the faith to pagan lands, our hearts begin to be fired with a zealous desire to do something for the salvation of our neighbor, but how can we reach him? "Oh!" we often think, "if we could bring but one soul to God!" We can; each one of us can save one soul—his own; and that is also a soul created to the image and likeness of the Holy Trinity, a soul ransomed by the Blood of Christ; it is the one which God most particularly desires that each one shall bring to Him. Think of that! Is not that alone an inestimable privilege? Should we not be very careful how we, even for that which we might imagine would bring salvation to another, put in peril the eternal welfare of that precious trust? But while we are effecting our own salvation, cannot we do something to assist in the rescue of others from everlasting perdition? Yes; certainly we can. Without leaving her cottage, Louise, through her sufferings, reaches the whole world, bringing down fertilizing showers of grace on hearts rendered sterile by sin; in her we see as true zeal for the conversion of sinners as that which filled the heart of St. Francis Xavier, and we learn from her that, without endeavoring to employ weapons in the use of which we are not only unskilled, but which, perhaps, would endanger our own salvation, we can, by simply offering up to God the trials which He sends us, do a great deal for the spiritual welfare of others, without quitting that station in which God Himself has placed us. The zeal which these victims of expiation and the great apostles of the faith exhibit is always characterized by thorough disinterestedness; it is natural to desire the conversion of our friends, it is commendable, but—after all, it is only loving our neighbor as ourselves. To desire the repentance of all sinners throughout the whole world, just because God created them to serve Him, just because Christ redeemed them, is to love God above all things, and our neighbor in Him and for His sake.

Can we leave Louise and not carry away a deep impression of the dignity of sorrow? Do not her wounds send forth a glory that illuminates all the misfortunes of life so that we can trace the stigmata imprinted on every style of suffering? And when we have thus seen these sacred characters adorning affliction, can we ever fall into the pagan error of regarding the unfortunate as beings accursed by God, and delivered over to the power of the devil? Will we still consider that wherever the Church is persecuted, it must be because there its members have proved recreant to their duty? Will we not learn that whenever the faithful are cast into prison, or in any way deprived of religious liberty, it is because God makes of them victims of expiation to atone for the neglect of other Christians, will not the trials of Catholic nations recall to our minds the stripes and imprisonment suffered by St. Paul, who declared that he refused all glory save that of the cross? Ever since the day on which the Passion of Our Lord converted the Roman gibbet, the symbol of the lowest infamy, into the honored emblem of salvation, Calvary has set its royal seal of the Cross on every affliction that befalls the human race; beneath this seal, if we examine closely, we will find the stigmata—that is, some peculiar attribute of the Passion—more or less clearly defined. Bodily pain bears the stigmata so visibly that all must therein acknowledge their presence—for example, who can suffer the racking torture of a headache and not recall the Crown of Thorns?

In that class of suffering which afflicts our minds and our hearts we find the stigmata even more deeply impressed. Are we undeservedly the victims of treacherous conduct, do our best friends desert us in our hour of need?—that is the shadow of Gethsemani; and Gethsemani is but Calvary anticipated. Does a curious complication of circumstances, or a series of artful calumnies contrive to present you in a false light to your spiritual superiors, so that nothing but a miracle could enable you to remove the impression that has been produced; remember that here, too, you find the stigmata. Christ was condemned to be delivered to the authorities by the priests of a hierarchy established by His own Father. In how many ways the Church, the spouse of Christ, has received the stigmata! False accusations seem to be her portion; is it strange that men should dare to cast upon her the imputation of disturbing public peace, public order, when her Divine Spouse, the Creator of peace and order, was accused of arousing sedition among the people? When He, by whose Almighty power Cæsar held his dominions, was called a foe to Cæsar's rights? Perhaps the tide of popular opinion brands you without reason as a malefactor, perhaps the angry multitude are clamorous for an unjust sentence to be pronounced upon you —do you not hear the echo of "Away with

Him! Crucify Him!" As to social degradation, there was enough of that, both on Calvary and all along the weary road that led to it. The Passion was nothing but degradation from beginning to end; yet God the Father chose it for the Son and the Word of God left the Bosom of the Father that He might add to the ocean of His own unapproachable glory by means of this degradation, as St. Mary Magdalen Pazzi tells us with the authority of the dying: "Know that the exercise of suffering is a thing so glorious and noble that the Word who found in the Bosom of His eternal Father the most abundant riches and joys of Paradise, because He was not decorated with the stole of suffering, came on earth to seek this ornament, and He was God who cannot be deceived." There are none except the very holy who can resolve to seek humiliations, and God does not require that of us, but when He offers them to us, we can recognize the honor of being called to the Right Hand by a path similar to that which Christ chose for Himself. Could we ask for better than that which God chose for His only begotten Son? Is there a better way? "He was God, who cannot be deceived."

There is nothing save sin that is really debasing, though the world may tell us differently. It is not to its maxims, however, that Christians should harken. Are you obliged to perform tasks beyond your strength, below your rank? He who as man was prince of a royal house—He for whose very sake the sceptre had been given to Juda—bore the weight of a huge cross up a long ascent, all the more fatiguing because imperceptible, and this burden had been hitherto laid on only the vilest of criminals. Nor must we, in the midst of the sufferings of Calvary, lose sight of Our Blessed Lady, for as Blessed Robert Malatesta received the Five Wounds, not from Our Lord Himself, but at the hand of St. Francis of Assisi, so we may receive from her some of the stigmata of that Passion in which she so closely participated. When parents linger beside what they fear may be the deathbed of one of their children, when a mother sees her child enduring the torture of some frightful malady, sinking beneath the ravages of unconquerable disease, this is the stigmata of Her of whom the Church speaks when she chants

> Stabat Mater dolorosa
> Juxta crucem—

Poverty bears the stigmata almost as visibly as did her bridegroom, St. Francis, for she reigned supreme on that real Good Friday which accomplished our Redemption, and who can covet riches after Our Lord denied Himself the right to bequeath even his garments to His Mother? when He made Himself so poor that an outcast, by virtue of the manner of His death, from the tomb of His ancestors. He was dependant on the bounty of another for a tomb. And if, although we desire to be resigned, we sometimes cry aloud beneath the load of accumulated afflictions, we need not be disheartened; these exclamations only indicate that sorrow is performing its appointed task, and in this utter desolation of spirit we again find the stigmata, for Christ on the Cross lamented aloud that He was forsaken by all, even by His Father.

XI.

HAD we hoped to find oblivion in sleep when we retired to rest the night of Friday, September 18, 1874, we would have discovered that our anticipations were vain; Louise was as distinctly before us as she had been while we were kneeling in her cottage. More clear than our dreams, totally distinct and separate from them, her figure never left our minds throughout the hours of that night, and many days had elapsed when this vision at last ceased to be ever present. It is now three full years since we saw Louise, but we can at will recall all the events of that scene, and whenever her name is mentioned we seem to see her as we saw her then.

No need of the slightest sound to arouse us the next morning, and the first signs of daylight found us on the highway leading to Bois d'Haine. How earnestly we wished that neither Louise nor her sisters would notice us as we passed their house, for we hoped to conceal ourselves behind the pillars in the church, so that we would not attract the attention of anyone, and thus secure a chance of seeing Louise approach the Holy Table when she was not aware of the presence of strangers, but these hopes were to be disappointed. Just as we drew near to Louise's home, the door opened, and a little woman, dressed in black, hurriedly tying her cap strings with hands whose fingers could not be excelled in nimbleness, tripped down the steps, and we were face to face with Louise herself. No need to glance at the black mittens for the assurance of the fact—it was none other save the Stigmatica. She was pale, not with the pallor of sickness, but with the hue of one who dwells in another world; many have written of the unredeemed ugliness of Louise's countenance at ordinary times, and the doctor's impression had prepared us for just nothing but a peasant girl; but as she then appeared, her features, though ill-formed, were expressive of a certain dignity, and they were animated by a spiritual beauty not of this life. Can she ever really indulge in thoughtless merriment? Was it not an amiable condescension that she was practicing when the doctor first saw her? Was it not an example of the manner in which the Saints of God have often sought to screen the greatness of the heavenly favors which they receive by common-place actions?

Louise looked at us for a second, and, turning, she fled like a startled fawn in the direction of the railway. We had several times been told of her peculiar gait, and now we saw to full advantage how, with her whole person thrown forward, she appeared rather borne along by wings than by those quick-springing footsteps that seemed scarcely to touch the ground.

When she had almost reached the railway, she met a peasant lad, to whom she addressed some questions, which we did not hear. The boy instantly bared his head, and had an angel descended from on high to greet him he could not have replied with more respect and awe. Passing over the railway tracks, Louise disappeared in the house of the family employed in guarding the crossing of the highway with the railroad, and we never saw her again.

Not having witnessed her reception of Holy Communion in the Church, we find it difficult to believe the majority of those who have written concerning her, when they tell us that it was wholly unmarked by ecstasy; and when we consider that all unite in saying that, although what is related of Louise is so beyond comprehension, there is much that is wonderful of which we are told nothing, we are inclined to think that perhaps those who would really see Louise at the Holy Table would find her in ecstasy. Why she exhibited so much fear at meeting us seems inexplicable; perhaps it was merely the effect of the supernatural shame with which she is afflicted. Perhaps her subsequent non-appearance at Mass, or at least her absence from the body of the Church and from the Holy Table might be explained by informing us that the presence of strangers in the church was allowed by a Divine dispensation intended for the preservation of her humility, to hamper her devotions, to restrain her acts of thanksgiving, and to deprive her of the consolations of ecstasy. This is but a surmise; if the readers can think of another solution of this mystery they are certainly at liberty to prefer it.

That morning we were in one sense disappointed, but we did see the evidences of Louise's health and strength in a manner which we had not expected, and we witnessed enough while at Bois d'Haine to be able to echo with all our hearts the words of one possessing an intellect greater than any one of ours, who exclaimed, after visiting Maria Mörl, "I came, I saw, and—I believed."

THE END.

INDEX OR RECAPITULATION.

	PAGE.
Louise Lateau was born January 30, 1850,	66
Made her first Communion at the age of eleven years,	69
Began to earn her living as a seamstress at the age of fifteen,	69
The conduct of Louise during the Cholera of 1866—she devotes herself to the pest stricken,	71
Louise, attacked in 1867 by a lingering malady, receives the last Sacraments,	76
She is cured miraculously, but only for a short time,	76
She first experienced pain in the locality of the Stigmata on the first Friday of 1868,	77
She received the last Sacraments again at the close of Holy Week, 1868,	78
She then foretold her recovery, and was, on April 21, 1868, suddenly restored to health,	79
The first outward indication of the Stigmata took place on Friday, April 24, 1868,	88
The wound in the side was then visible; it healed the next day,	88
Friday, May 1st, blood issued from the upper surfaces of her feet, as well as from her side; she then confided the matter to M. le Curé,	88
May 8th, the Stigmata of the hands added themselves to the others; M. le Curé advised her to apply to the physician of Fayt, who attempted to cure her,	88
First evidences of ecstasy shown by Louise during the summer of 1867; marks of ecstasy also noticed by her friends during Holy Week, 1868,	92
Her first decided ecstasy took place July 17, 1868,	93
Her crown of thorns first appeared Friday, Sept. 25, 1868,	98
After this she ceased to sleep,	102
Her complete abstinence from all nourishment began March 30, 1871,	103
The wound on the shoulder appeared April 4, 1873,	107
Her ecstasy on Friday, September 18, 1874,	201
Her health on Saturday, September 19, 1874,	266

www.ingramcontent.com/pod-product-compliance
Lightning Source LLC
Chambersburg PA
CBHW052213240426
43670CB00037B/429